D1369990

The Unfinished Agenda
of
Brown v. Board of Education

The Editors of *Black Issues in Higher Education*

with

James Anderson, Ph.D.

and Dara N. Byrne, Ph.D.

LANDMARKS IN CIVIL RIGHTS HISTORY

WILEY

John Wiley & Sons, Inc.

This book is printed on acid-free paper. ∞

Published by John Wiley & Sons, Inc., Hoboken, New Jersey
Published simultaneously in Canada

Design and production by Navta Associates, Inc.

Photos pp. xv, 8–9, 98, 110–111, 127, 152, National Archives; p. xxi, photograph by William Cox; pp. 16, 21, 36, 51, 71, 82, 102, 103, 120, 131, 142, 158 by Ishmail Conway; p. 24, *New York World-Telegram and Sun* Photograph Collection, Library of Congress Prints and Photographs Division; p. 31, by Steven Early, courtesy of Tribune Media; pp. 78, 138, National Archives Middle Atlantic Region, Center City Philadelphia, PA; p. 108, Robert B. Honeyman Jr. Collection of Early Californian and Western American Pictorial, Bancroft Library, University of California, Berkeley; p. 124, by E. W. Clay, courtesy of Boondocksnet.com; p. 168, courtesy of Brown Foundation

Cartoons pp. 44, 62 by Melvin Tapley, courtesy of Melvin Tapley

Diagram p. 34, designed by Mark Bartley

For general information about our other products and services, please contact our Customer Care Department within the United States at (800) 762-2974, outside the United States at (317) 572-3993 or fax (317) 572-4002.

Wiley also publishes its books in a variety of electronic formats. Some content that appears in print may not be available in electronic books. For more information about Wiley products, visit our web site at www.wiley.com.

Library of Congress Cataloging-in-Publication Data:

The unfinished agenda of Brown v. Board of Education / the editors of Black issues in higher education with James Anderson and Dara N. Byrne.
    p. cm.
"Landmarks in civil rights history."
Includes bibliographical references and index.
  ISBN 0-471-64926-0 (cloth : alk. paper)
  1. Segregation in education—Law and legislation—United States—History. 2. Race discrimination—Law and legislation—United States—History. 3. African Americans—Civil rights—History. 4. Brown, Oliver, 1918—Trials, litigation, etc. I. Anderson, James, Ph. D. II. Byrne, Dara N. III. Black issues in higher education.
  KF4155.U54 2004
  344.73'0798—dc22

2003019753

Printed in the United States of America
10 9 8 7 6 5 4 3 2 1

This book is dedicated to my mother, Artensie Wesley Cox, a strong, independent, and caring woman who instilled in my brothers, my sister, and me a strong sense of values, spirituality, compassion, and love for all.

It is also dedicated to my granddaughter, Rhyann Lee Clark, who will someday examine *Brown v. Board of Education* in a much different light than those of us today. I trust that her life will be free of the trials that I and members of my generation of African Americans had to endure growing up and living in a rigid, segregated society in the United States of America.

Finally, it is dedicated to Miss Kisiah V. Autry and Mrs. Nellie Lee Elmore, my first educators. It was they who started me down the path of educational pursuits that I still travel today.

William E. Cox, *Black Issues in Higher Education*

To my dear wife and spiritual sister, Joan Morgan Matthews, with whom I gratefully participate in the greatest and most important education work of all: teaching others about the purpose of our creator Jehovah God and his son Jesus Christ as told in the Bible. Their assurance that our children, Maya and Franky, our grandsons, Jaylen and Matthew, as well as any right-hearted person can live in a world devoid of all problems, including those that gave rise to the *Brown* litigation, is the best lesson of all and a source of happiness beyond compare.

Frank L. Matthews, *Black Issues in Higher Education*

CONTENTS

A WORD FROM THEODORE M. SHAW OF THE NAACP LEGAL DEFENSE AND EDUCATIONAL FUND, INC.

The NAACP Legal Defense and Educational Fund, Inc. (LDF) is the nation's oldest legal organization fighting for equal rights under the law. Established in 1940 under the direction of the late Thurgood Marshall, the LDF initially was an independent litigation arm of the National Association for the Advancement of Colored People; the two groups separated entirely in 1957.

I never knew what it was like to live in a United States where the promise of equal protection under the law was meaningless. When I began practicing law, *Brown v. Board of Education* seemed to have been decided eons ago. I was born six months after the landmark Supreme Court decision, which struck down legally mandated public school segregation. Yet, the struggle against racial discrimination has been my life's work, and despite great progress, it seems as if there is enough work to last a lifetime.

Fifty years after *Brown,* the struggle continues. Due to the work of Charles Hamilton Houston, Thurgood Marshall, Robert Carter, Jack Greenberg, Constance Baker Motley, James Nabrit Jr., Oliver Hill, William T. Coleman, Louis Pollack, Charles Duncan, and others, *Brown* stands as one of our most important moments. But the work is not yet finished. As we commemorate *Brown v. Board of Education* and all we have accomplished since then, it is important to engage in a critical commemoration and then rededicate ourselves to the work that Thurgood Marshall and others began so long ago.

There is a song in the black church that says, "My soul looks back and wonders how I got over." I got over because of the civil rights movement and the demand for black empowerment. They opened doors that I do not think would ever have opened otherwise. My generation bore the brunt of the school desegregation battles, which continued into and through the 1970s. As a consequence of the work of the LDF, the Justice Department, and the NAACP, by the late 1970s things began to change for many schoolchildren. However, in the 1980s, the era of school desegregation was brought to a halt and then turned around. By the early 1990s schools districts that were once segregated were operating securely in the fiction that they now had broken the link between past *intentionally* segregative acts and present-day segregation.

In 1995, I argued *Missouri v. Jenkins,* the last school desegregation case decided by the Supreme Court. *Jenkins* was the last of the series of cases (1991's *Board of Education of Oklahoma v. Dowell,* and 1992's *Freeman v. Pitts*) in which the Court had signaled a retreat from its earlier cases implementing the *Brown v. Board* decision. In the course of oral argument Justice Anthony Kennedy asked me whether it was true that the primary purpose of the Court was to return the school district to local control. I responded affirmatively, adding "after the violation has been cured."

I have often thought about this exchange, because in my view it captured the core of two competing visions of desegregation cases: one sees segregation as an enduring effect of long-term discrimination that can only be undone by concerted and sustained action; the other sees the desegregation process as an unpleasant usurpation of authority that must be ended as soon as possible in order to return to the status quo.

In recent years, this cramped vision of the *Brown* mandate has coincided with the ideological argument that makes any intentional and voluntary attempt to address racial segregation and inequality comparable to racial discrimination against white people, conflating race consciousness with racism. The argument, which masquerades as "colorblindness," is posited against affirmative action and even voluntary school desegregation efforts. At its most notorious, the argument was manifested in the University of Michigan cases.

I taught at Michigan Law School from 1990 until 1993, and served on the faculty committee that drafted the admissions plan upheld by the Supreme Court in June 2003. We were faithful to the 1977 *University of California Regents v. Bakke* decision, then the only Supreme Court precedent, in adopting a policy in which race was considered as one factor among many in pursuit of broad diversity without quotas or separate admissions pools. We did not draft a program with the intent or the effect of illegally discriminating against and disadvantaging white students. Despite attempts of our adversaries to distort the facts, ignore history, and stand principle on its head, whatever the merits of the affirmative action debate, there is no moral or legal equivalent between affirmative action and invidious discrimination.

In the Michigan undergraduate case, I served as lead counsel for black and Latino students who were full parties to the litigation. We made the argument that affirmative action is justified not only by colleges and universities' First Amendment interest in selecting a diverse student body, but also by minority students' Fourteenth Amendment interest in remedying the effects of a long history of discrimination and exclusion.

Michigan, like *Brown,* was a milepost, not an end point. As important a victory as it was—and it was enormous—there is a bigger storm brewing. Scholarships, mentoring, pipeline, internship, and leadership programs for black and brown students are all in the crosshairs of radical conservatives. At issue today is whether it is illegal to consciously and voluntarily take any action aimed at ameliorating racial inequality; if race-conscious programs targeted at minority groups are declared illegal, all of these programs fall.

So, as we commemorate *Brown,* despite great progress, we continue the ongoing struggle against racial discrimination.

The stakes could not be higher.

Theodore M. Shaw
President and Director-Counsel

COMMEMORATING *BROWN* ON THE TWENTIETH ANNIVERSARY OF *BLACK ISSUES IN HIGHER EDUCATION*

Frank L. Matthews

It is quite fitting and appropriate that the *Brown* decision and *Black Issues in Higher Education* hold concurrent anniversary observances. It truly can be said that *Black Issues* had its genesis with *Brown.* Had it not been for its legacy, we would not have had the opportunity to "go for it" back in 1983 when we thought ours was an idea whose time had come.

Over the past twenty years *Black Issues* has grown from a four-page black-and-white newsletter to the most widely read news journal of its type in the United States. We have brought our readers exclusive interviews from every U.S. secretary of education to discussions on retention and recruitment of minority faculty. Our subscribers range from those on death row to those who frequent the White House. We have represented viewpoints ranging from high school dropouts to Nobel laureates. Educational issues continue to be the great common denominator in American society.

Black Issues gave new meaning to the phrase *educational accountability* when we introduced the Top 100 report which fast became the standard for objectively gauging and documenting how U.S. colleges rate in graduating African Americans and other students of color.

The rich legacy of Arthur Ashe Jr. lives through our annual report bearing his name. This report profiles thousands of students of color who have outstanding accomplishments both in the classroom and in athletic competition.

We've chronicled the heartfelt deeds of wonderful people like Oseola McCarty, the maid from Mississippi, whose meager income resulted in the stuff of philanthropic legend; Bill and Camille Cosby, whose generous gift to Spelman College is still unmatched; and Bill and Melinda Gates, who raised the minority scholarship ante to the billion-dollar range.

In 1989, we developed a live, interactive videoconference that gave participants on college campuses the opportunity to engage with prominent members of the education and business communities, as well as government and political officials. *Beyond the Dream, A Celebration of Black History,* was our first videoconference, and now this annual program is recognized as the national kickoff to Black History Month.

Any successful venture, however, owes an immense debt of gratitude to the many professionals who have given so much over the years. We have been blessed to have been associated with some of the hardest working and most dedicated people who can be found. The news stories and issues that they have brought to you have ranged from the uplifting accounts of students who successfully matriculated against seemingly insurmountable odds to the brave and self sacrificing leaders who have given so much to insuring that educational access and parity be a reality for millions of traditionally disenfranchised students.

We have come to take pride in our reputation for fair but tough reporting. In 2002 *Black Issues* won the coveted Folio award as the outstanding educational publication in the United States. This award only served to confirm what our many faithful and loyal readers already knew: *Black Issues* is an indispensable part of the higher education landscape.

On behalf of all of our current and former colleagues and associates we sincerely thank you, our loyal subscribers, advertisers, and supporters, for the privilege of twenty years of service to you.

Supreme Court of the United States

No. 1 ———, *October Term, 19* 54

Oliver Brown, Mrs. Richard Lawton, Mrs. Sadie Emmanuel et al.,
Appellants,

vs.

Board of Education of Topeka, Shawnee County, Kansas, et al.

Appeal from *the United States District Court for the* ———————————
District of Kansas.

This cause *came on to be heard on the transcript of the record from the United States*
District Court for the ———————— *District of* Kansas, ————————
and was argued by counsel.

On consideration whereof, *It is ordered and adjudged by this Court that the judgment*
of the said District ———————— *Court in this cause be, and the same is*
hereby, reversed with costs; and that this cause be, and the same
is hereby, remanded to the said District Court to take such
proceedings and enter such orders and decrees consistent with
the opinions of this Court as are necessary and proper to admit
to public schools on a racially nondiscriminatory basis with all
deliberate speed the parties to this case.

Per Mr. Chief Justice Warren,

May 31, 1955.

1469

Brown v. Board decision

XV

REFLECTIONS OF ONE
WHO WAS THERE

WILLIAM E. COX

I look at the *Brown v. Board of Education* decision by the Supreme Court of the United States in 1954 through a different lens from most Americans. My perspective may not even be shared by the majority of African Americans who have felt the beneficial impact of *Brown* over the past half century, because I am a black man who was born, raised, educated, and had my career roots in the Deep South during the era of "separate but equal," a phenomenon that can best be described as a hoax.

I experienced segregation firsthand. It was not something my elders shared with me—not something I read about in a novel or a history book. I lived segregation. Mention segregated lunch counters, water fountains, restrooms, and schools, and I can take you there. My memories of those experiences are as vivid and poignant as if they happened yesterday.

Life in Bay Minette, Alabama, in post–World War II America was very much like life in other parts of the Deep South. Even though the war between the North and the South had ended some eighty years before, the segregation of people by the color of their skin was still the prevailing custom of the times.

Signs that directed "colored" to another entrance to a restaurant (often a take-out window in the rear) or bathroom is a vivid memory to me. I saw those signs in my community and everywhere I was willing to travel in my boyhood and adolescence. I say willing to travel, because blacks in the Deep South knew they were taking certain risks each time they ventured beyond both the visible and invisible borders that had been placed there by those wanting to separate the races.

When I started school in 1948, my first year was spent in a two-room building, Pine Grove Grammar School, in Bay Minette, that held twenty students. Segregated for the many years that it existed, that building housed six grades taught by two teachers—three grades each. That building is etched in my memory. Little if any care ever went into its maintenance. A paintbrush probably had never touched the structure. But it was the very first place I called school. I thought my first-grade teacher, Miss Kisiah V. Autry, was the smartest person in the world. In fact, she did not even have a college degree but had achieved about as much education as blacks could achieve in those days of crushing oppression. Miss Autry continued to pursue her studies each summer and eventually obtained her baccalaureate degree and met the certification standards set by the state of Alabama for teachers. The second person who had a significant educational impact on my life was Mrs. Nellie Lee Elmore, who also served as the teacher/supervisor of that small school for black children in Baldwin County; some would say that her position was the equivalent of superintendent of schools. I mention this about her title and responsibilities because, after the closing of Pine Grove Grammar School, she was not allowed to perform administrative duties or assume an educational leadership role in the white school system. Like so many black educational leaders of her day, she was assigned classroom-teaching duties in an elementary school when the changes resulting from *Brown* slowly began to take effect.

The black students attending segregated schools had few clues as to how different their education was from that of the white children going to school down the road a few miles. I didn't know that my textbooks were the used textbooks of others, that our science and athletic equipment represented the hand-me-downs of the other schools in the district.

I attended that small grammar school for only one year before it closed. I went on to a larger school—Douglasville High School. Still segregated, it was a larger facility serving a broader community of black students. Our two teachers joined a much larger faculty. Twenty students now joined approximately three hundred. But most of my educational experiences remained inferior to those being enjoyed by white students in the community, the state of Alabama, and the nation.

My classmates and I had limited opportunities and challenging boundaries that restricted us from moving too far away from our homes and families. Few black youth of the 1950s and early 1960s in Alabama or other places in the Deep South could expect to see their education going much beyond a high school diploma. And many didn't even achieve that milestone. My classmates and I struggled to succeed and received little attention for our special needs. Those who succeeded in attaining a diploma had few paths to follow upon graduating. My sole first-grade classmate at Pine Grove Grammar School became pregnant and dropped out in her teens—a path repeated by far too many young women of the time. Unemployment or underemployment was far more prevalent than postsecondary education and career opportunities.

I didn't comprehend that our teachers—as committed, energetic, and caring as they were—were measured by a different yardstick of professional preparation. It never dawned on me that per-pupil expenditures for black students in Bay Minette were only a small percentage of that spent for whites. Because of the boundaries that restricted so many young blacks, few of us knew then about the incredible world of educational and career opportunities that existed beyond our immediate world.

Those less than ideal conditions did not hinder a significant number of individuals from achieving in school and continuing on to success in a myriad of career endeavors. Their individual accomplishments are a testament to the power of the person and his will to succeed. They met the challenges brought on by the inequities of segregation and made the most of the educational experiences afforded them.

Included among my student associates at Douglasville High School was Henry Sanders, who went on to acquire a law degree from Harvard University and is serving with distinction in the Senate of the state of Alabama. Clarence Gardner earned a Ph.D. in engineering and enjoyed a successful career as a U.S. Air Force officer. John Carter became a successful high school principal in Camden, Alabama, while Janice Anderson Inge and Eloise Watson Gardner committed their lives and careers to teaching in the school systems of Los Angeles, California, and Mobile, Alabama, respectively.

The city of Baton Rouge, Louisiana, benefited from the talents of Jerald Boykin, an alumnus who went on to become assistant to the mayor and director of personnel for Louisiana's capital city. And Mattie Harris Hardy brought honor to students attending Faulkner State College, where she served as a student services professional. Many of my peers are serving as ministers, health care professionals, and entrepreneurs in towns and cities across Alabama and the nation. Their common denominator was that they rose from a segregated education in the United States and made the most of their futures in the worlds of business, military, government, education, and an array of different settings.

Life away from school embodied experiences that I'm certain I shared with many of my peers. My father, Jesse Cox, died when I was ten years old and I was raised by a very loving, hardworking mother. A deeply religious woman, Artensie Cox provided for us through her maid service to white families in the Bay Minette community, pursuits that she continued until age eighty-two.

My mother was not an educated woman in the "book sense," but she possessed a work ethic and value system that gave solid direction to my three siblings and me. We knew we were loved, and we were taught the meaning of right and wrong. My mother, through what we would today call "parenting skills," taught me self-reliance—that what I was going to achieve, I was going to have to work very hard for. She believed that a good education was the route to a good career and a better life. She introduced me to values that were reinforced by the strong educators with whom I had the good fortune to study, in school and later in college. She was not financially able to send me to college, but she helped. I had to work for $3\frac{1}{2}$ of my college years, until graduation.

While the specific opportunities being denied to black students were unknown to me at the time, the boundaries were eminently clear. From my mother, I learned about the borders that existed in the segregated South and the dangers associated with getting too close to or cross-

Pine Grove Grammar School

ing them. I learned where to travel and what behaviors to display in which environments. The geographic boundaries were the easy ones. I knew what section of Bay Minette I could be in at what time of the day and night. I also learned the consequences a young black man could face if he violated those boundaries.

From my life experiences, my family, and those educators, I understood that if I wanted more out of life, education was the way to achieve it. I developed fairly lofty goals for a young man whose life experiences sheltered me from educational and career potential and hid from me effective expression of the gifts I possessed.

Alabama A&M, a historically black college in Huntsville, Alabama, was to eventually play an important role in my life. The "college on the hill" became for me what other historically black colleges and universities are to so many black Americans—a stepping-stone to the future.

I had never been on a college campus until the day I went to A&M for the first time. There was a sense of promise—of opportunity—that I recognized that first day. I knew if my life were to be different, education was going to play a major part in that change, and I "took" to college immediately. College was to be a major factor in my life.

My time at Alabama A&M extended my vision and expanded the mental map formed in my childhood and adolescent years. The more I saw and experienced, the larger and more comprehensive became my dreams.

Attending college in the early sixties was an incredible experience, the poignancy of which even a black person of another generation cannot fathom. Social and economic unrest was rampant. The civil rights movement was gaining impetus. Martin Luther King Jr., Medgar Evers, Malcolm X, and others were speaking out in voices that grew louder and louder. Marches, sit-ins, and other forms of civil disobedience became vehicles that angry blacks and others who supported our cause used to call attention to the inequity and injustice that resulted from discrimination.

This also was a time when racist values were being vociferously advanced by exponents such as Governors Orville Faubus and George Wallace and Senator Strom Thurmond. National television news was filled frequently with scenes of church burnings, Freedom Riders, and local law enforcement officers with German shepherd dogs blocking school entrances. Civil rights protests and racist reactions were not distant news to me. They were happening up the road and had a profound effect on my fellow A&M students and me. I am certain they also affected my fellow classmate Vivian Malone Jones, who transferred from Alabama A&M to the University of Alabama during the infamous "stand in the schoolhouse door." Vivian was one of the first African Americans to enroll in 1963. She graduated from the University of Alabama in 1965.

Those events heightened my resolve that getting a college degree would be my passport to something better than many blacks before me had experienced. It also was a time when I tested the prejudice that dictated what I was "allowed" to do and prohibited from doing. I questioned the rules that were unfair and oppressive, and I often got in trouble for my rebellion.

Alabama and the rest of the United States were experiencing change, some rapid, some slowed by those who resisted that change. Surviving during that time was hugely challenging. Thriving was even more difficult. The most successful people I discovered were those who blended their intellect, attributes, and ambition with opportunity. That is a formula I created for myself then—one I still apply to this day. *Brown,* though painfully slow to take real effect, had an impact on the third ingredient in that formula for success.

Armed with my baccalaureate degree from Alabama A&M in 1964, I signed on to work for the General Electric Company, where my first job was to perform design work on the Apollo spacecraft ground support system. That experience introduced me to a world much larger than Alabama.

Early in my career I moved from the private sector to government. My first assignment was with the U.S. Army, and still living in Alabama, I taught courses in electronic guidance missile systems operations at a U.S. military installation, Redstone Arsenal, in Alabama. This experience began my career in education. Soon my career as an educator took an abrupt turn, both in responsibility and life experience. I accepted an educational role as a mathematics, electronics, and general aeronautics instructor with the U.S. Armed Forces Institute and moved to Europe for my next teaching assignment. My work in Europe, first with the army and eventually the air force, gave me my first taste of educational administration as I became involved in the design and delivery of adult and postsecondary education programs at air bases in West Germany.

I stress my early career because I couldn't have entered or succeeded without my college degree, and had I not been willing to pull up my roots and travel halfway around the world to pursue my dreams. Few of my peers had that opportunity. I share my life experiences to put the times in perspective. Equality, while still far from fully realized, did not exist in any form in the America of my youth and young adulthood. The rights to vote and hold office, the right to all the privileges, and the opportunity to pursue a quality education and eventually gain access to the world of work were not characteristics of this nation in the middle of the twentieth century. Racism, discrimination, and prejudice were the rules.

When those brave individuals brought the *Brown* case to the judicial halls of this nation, they were arguing for issues that should have been won half a century before, but the previous argument had been lost to opponents of equality who instituted the farce of "separate but equal."

Fifty years after the Supreme Court decision of 1954 that initiated significant change in the American education system for blacks, segregation in this nation still wreaks havoc in all levels of education. And while it took years for states to take action based on the *Brown* decision, without the Court ruling segregation perhaps would have continued for years to come. Still, despite numerous battles—in the Supreme Court and other courts—issues remain on who is admitted to which schools, based on the color of their skin.

Shameful acts and outright racism continue to exist. Today, public schools, especially those in large urban areas, are as segregated as they were prior to the *Brown* decision. The difference is that fifty years ago segregation was a result of a decision to keep black and white children separated; today it is due to the flight of whites from urban areas.

While *Brown v. Board of Education* was a precedent-setting decision and is viewed as a turning point in U.S. social history, it was not a thunderous explosion that rocked the foundation of discrimination. Rather, it was a "law of the land" lever that civil rights advocates could use. The real change took place on many fronts, hard won by many people. The changes that brought us where we are today have had a "melting pot" of contributors. Every community added its own advocates, and together they became formidable as a force advancing change in the United States.

Black Issues in Higher Education is my way of joining the myriad contributors in the continuing effort to change education in the United States, not only to provide access for African Americans and others who have been denied it, but also to increase the quality of education for the entire nation. I trust that this book will be a testimony to the hard-won gains and a trumpet call for the battles still to be waged.

PREFACE

Looking Back, Looking Forward: Reading *The Unfinished Agenda*

JAMES ANDERSON AND DARA N. BYRNE

The *Black Issues in Higher Education* editorial team had a very broad audience in mind when we put this book together. We thought about a readership who might range from those who may not know anything about the case to those who may have more specialized knowledge. We were committed to creating a widely accessible book because we feel that a deep understanding of the impact of *Brown* is essential to continue the efforts toward full citizenship for all Americans. *Brown* was an item on that larger agenda. *The Unfinished Agenda* offers enlightening chapters on themes that make up this landmark case and provides a lens through which to view race relations and education in America today.

These chapters are not meant to be definitive; they are to serve as reflections on the profound transformation of the United States over the past fifty years. We asked ten scholars, researchers, and writers from very diverse backgrounds to share their perspectives. To view *Brown* solely through a legal lens ignores its profound reverberations. To examine only the educational and social outcomes attributed to *Brown* ignores the responsibility of the courts and the legal system. To appreciate the impact and significance of *Brown* over a fifty-year span of segregation-desegregation-resegregation in American education, a wide variety of voices had to be represented, including visionaries who participated in the *Brown* decision.

The strength of this book is its focus on the relationships between core issues and tangential arguments about the decision. The chapters are intentionally interpretive. The contributors have rendered some of the most provocative and insightful analyses available on the topic.

Kahlil Chism's chapter serves as a detailed and much-needed overview of the case. Chism's piece anchors every other chapter in this book and brings the timeline found on page xxxiii to life.

Juan Williams's chapter on the attorneys details the legal strategy developed by former dean of Howard University School of Law Charles Hamilton Houston and the NAACP Legal Defense Fund. Williams shows us Thurgood Marshall up close, his posture in the courtroom, and how he won over an all-white Supreme Court. The legal analysis provided by Charles Ogletree's chapter makes sense of the cases leading up to *Brown* while also explaining recent cases that have all but reversed the impact of *Brown* in the courts. The legal mind of Ms. Geneva Crenshaw in Derrick Bell's chapter will certainly intrigue. A straightforward and easy-to-follow dialogue that examines several important legal cases, Bell's chapter considers what might have happened if *Brown* had been lost.

Mary Futrell's chapter gives extensive detail about the role desegregation played in the waning presence of black teachers while also showing that the rise of blacks to top decision-making positions in education could not have been possible without *Brown*. Futrell's argument is solid, but her reflections on her experience as a teacher during this period form the heart of the chapter.

Richard Wright's chapter uses sociolinguistic methods to explore the hidden meanings behind the language in the decision. The chapter simplifies some rather complex analytical tools to provide an easy-to-follow interpretation of the use of terminology such as "separate but equal."

The *Black Issues* editorial team made a special effort to include perspectives from other communities that have been impacted by *Brown*. The legacy of struggle against racism, segregation, and equal access to education in the Asian American and Latino communities is discussed in the riveting chapters written by Evelyn Hu-DeHart and Marco Portales. Hu-DeHart's comparative analysis of Asian American students demystifies the "virtue" of the model minority label given to Asians everywhere.

A. Wade Boykin and James Jones's chapter is the perfect overlap for Hu-DeHart's and Portales' chapters. Boykin and Jones survey the major approaches to black children's education today, but the centerpiece of their argument is the psychological impact of diversity on all children.

Significantly, Gary Orfield's chapter at the close of this book calls to our attention the need for renewing our commitment to movement-building and political change to finish the work started so many years ago.

We also wanted to make the lived experience of *Brown* available to our readers. Ishmail Conway was asked to interview several people who were involved with the case, and the results of his and other interviews are the Voices of the Era pieces throughout. These firsthand reflections of experiences during segregation are legacies, and it would have been unwise to ignore these voices. We feel privileged to include them.

There is great power and pain in all the personal stories about *Brown* that have been tucked away for the past fifty years in the collective consciousness of those who waged a valiant struggle for educational equality for black children in the United States. The remarkable common thread is that each group of activists sought relief from oppression and access to opportunity, even under dire circumstances, by challenging the law. These narratives serve as valuable benchmarks for continued analysis of the unfinished agenda in post-*Brown* America.

The core issues addressed in *The Unfinished Agenda* constitute areas of contentious debate. It is impossible to cover them fully, and it has been a challenge looking back and looking forward with a critical eye. There is much to read and much to understand about *Brown,* and we trust that *The Unfinished Agenda* will spur you to begin your own fiftieth-anniversary reflection.

About Voices of the Era

Many of the sidebar narratives in this volume are drawn from Ishmail Conway's interviews with plaintiffs, attorneys, teachers, students, and activists involved in the *Brown v. Board of Education* case. This is but a small collection of oral histories related to this historic decision in the Supreme Court and in earlier decisions in lower courts.

It was not an easy task to conduct these interviews because many of the living plaintiffs, attorneys, and leaders are infirm. Regrettably, one of the Delaware plaintiffs, the Rev. Shirley Bulah Stamps, had a fatal heart attack the day before the scheduled interview.

Recording these oral histories was a group effort. Researchers from the Smithsonian Institution Museum, the National Archives, the Brown Foundation, Howard University, Washburn University, Delaware State University, and a host of others from the plaintiffs' five states assisted in making valuable archival information available. Five of the narratives were recorded in Washington, D.C., at the historic "Voices of the Legacy: Dialogue and Remembrances," the first session of the Brown Presidential Commission. Many of those interviewed revealed others in their communities who had stories about *Brown.* For example, Topeka plaintiff Zelma Henderson suggested that Mr. Merrill Ross be added to the list. Mr. Ross, a former Tuskegee airman, was the only Negro principal in Topeka in 1954.

The narratives represent the essence of each interviewee's story and provide added insight for *The Unfinished Agenda* from lived experiences.

The following is a list of Voices of the Era contained in this book:

ACKNOWLEDGMENTS

The *Black Issues in Higher Education* editorial team had a very broad audience in mind when we put this book together. We thought about a readership who might range from those who may not know anything about the case to those who may have more specialized knowledge. We were committed to creating a widely accessible book because we feel that a deep understanding of the impact of *Brown* is essential to continue the efforts toward full citizenship for all Americans. *Brown* was an item on that larger agenda. *The Unfinished Agenda* offers enlightening chapters on themes that make up this landmark case and provides a lens through which to view race relations and education in America today.

These chapters are not meant to be definitive; they are to serve as reflections on the profound transformation of the United States over the past fifty years. We asked ten scholars, researchers, and writers from very diverse backgrounds to share their perspectives. To view *Brown* solely through a legal lens ignores its profound reverberations. To examine only the educational and social outcomes attributed to *Brown* ignores the responsibility of the courts and the legal system. To appreciate the impact and significance of *Brown* over a fifty-year span of segregation-desegregation-resegregation in American education, a wide variety of voices had to be represented, including visionaries who participated in the *Brown* decision.

The strength of this book is its focus on the relationships between core issues and tangential arguments about the decision. The chapters are intentionally interpretive. The contributors have rendered some of the most provocative and insightful analyses available on the topic.

Kahlil Chism's chapter serves as a detailed and much-needed overview of the case. Chism's piece anchors every other chapter in this book and brings the timeline found on page xxxiii to life.

Juan Williams's chapter on the attorneys details the legal strategy developed by former dean of Howard University School of Law Charles Hamilton Houston and the NAACP Legal Defense Fund. Williams shows us Thurgood Marshall up close, his posture in the courtroom, and how he won over an all-white Supreme Court. The legal analysis provided by Charles Ogletree's chapter makes sense of the cases leading up to *Brown* while also explaining recent cases that have all but reversed the impact of *Brown* in the courts. The legal mind of Ms. Geneva Crenshaw in Derrick Bell's chapter will certainly intrigue. A straightforward and easy-to-follow dialogue that examines several important legal cases, Bell's chapter considers what might have happened if *Brown* had been lost.

Mary Futrell's chapter gives extensive detail about the role desegregation played in the waning presence of black teachers while also showing that the rise of blacks to top decision-making positions in education could not have been possible without *Brown*. Futrell's argument is solid, but her reflections on her experience as a teacher during this period form the heart of the chapter.

Richard Wright's chapter uses sociolinguistic methods to explore the hidden meanings behind the language in the decision. The chapter simplifies some rather complex analytical tools to provide an easy-to-follow interpretation of the use of terminology such as "separate but equal."

The *Black Issues* editorial team made a special effort to include perspectives from other communities that have been impacted by *Brown*. The legacy of struggle against racism, segregation, and equal access to education in the Asian American and Latino communities is discussed in the riveting chapters written by Evelyn Hu-DeHart and Marco Portales. Hu-DeHart's comparative analysis of Asian American students demystifies the "virtue" of the model minority label given to Asians everywhere.

A. Wade Boykin and James Jones's chapter is the perfect overlap for Hu-DeHart's and Portales' chapters. Boykin and Jones survey the major approaches to black children's education today, but the centerpiece of their argument is the psychological impact of diversity on all children.

Significantly, Gary Orfield's chapter at the close of this book calls to our attention the need for renewing our commitment to movement-building and political change to finish the work started so many years ago.

We also wanted to make the lived experience of *Brown* available to our readers. Ishmail Conway was asked to interview several people who were involved with the case, and the results of his and other interviews are the Voices of the Era pieces throughout. These firsthand reflections of experiences during segregation are legacies, and it would have been unwise to ignore these voices. We feel privileged to include them.

There is great power and pain in all the personal stories about *Brown* that have been tucked away for the past fifty years in the collective consciousness of those who waged a valiant struggle for educational equality for black children in the United States. The remarkable common thread is that each group of activists sought relief from oppression and access to opportunity, even under dire circumstances, by challenging the law. These narratives serve as valuable benchmarks for continued analysis of the unfinished agenda in post-*Brown* America.

The core issues addressed in *The Unfinished Agenda* constitute areas of contentious debate. It is impossible to cover them fully, and it has been a challenge looking back and looking forward with a critical eye. There is much to read and much to understand about *Brown,* and we trust that *The Unfinished Agenda* will spur you to begin your own fiftieth-anniversary reflection.

About Voices of the Era

Many of the sidebar narratives in this volume are drawn from Ishmail Conway's interviews with plaintiffs, attorneys, teachers, students, and activists involved in the *Brown v. Board of Education* case. This is but a small collection of oral histories related to this historic decision in the Supreme Court and in earlier decisions in lower courts.

TIMELINE FOR *BROWN V. BOARD OF EDUCATION*

1857: The Supreme Court rules in *Dred Scott v. Sandford* that neither free nor enslaved blacks have constitutional rights in the United States.

1863: January 1, President Abraham Lincoln signs the Emancipation Proclamation, which frees nearly 4 million slaves.

1865: March 3, Establishment of the Bureau of Refugees, Freedmen, and Abandoned Lands, the first federal welfare agency established to provide relief for free blacks and poor whites during the Civil War era.

1866: Passage of the Civil Rights Act of 1866.

1867: Howard University is established; this school would eventually train the majority of the NAACP Legal Defense Fund team.

1868: Passage and ratification of the Fourteenth Amendment.

1896: *Plessy v. Ferguson* establishes the doctrine of "separate but equal."

1935: Charles Hamilton Houston, along with former student Thurgood Marshall, begins challenging segregation laws in graduate and professional schools.

1938: *State of Missouri ex. rel. Gaines v. Canada* establishes that black students have the right to attend state-funded graduate facilities if no separate and equal facilities are available.

1948: The NAACP devotes efforts to an all-out attack on segregation in education.

1949: The NAACP files *Briggs v. Elliott* in Clarendon County, South Carolina.

1950: Charles Hamilton Houston files *Bolling v. Sharpe* in the District of Columbia. The Supreme Court hands down favorable rulings on *Sweatt v. Painter* and *McLaurin v. Oklahoma State Regents,* two graduate school admissions cases that help pave the way for *Brown.* Charles Hamilton Houston, the chief architect of the NAACP legal strategy, dies.

1951: Charles Scott, John Scott, and Robert Carter file *Brown v. Board of Education of Topeka* in February. Spottswood Robinson files *Davis v. Prince Edward County, Virginia,* in May. *Briggs v. Elliott* goes to trial in May. *Gebhart v. Belton* and *Gebhart v. Bulah* go to trial in October. Robert Carter and Charles Scott lead the first trial phase of *Brown v. Board of Education of Topeka* in June.

1952: In October the Supreme Court announces it will hear all five cases collectively; segregation in the public schools is presented as a national issue.

1953: Chief Justice Vinson dies. Earl Warren replaces Vinson as interim chief justice.

1954: On May 17 the Supreme Court unanimously rules that state-sanctioned segregation of public schools is a violation of the Fourteenth Amendment and is unconstitutional.

1955: Justice Jackson dies. He is replaced by John Marshall Harlan, grandson of the lone dissenter in *Plessy v. Ferguson.*

1955: The Supreme Court hands down *Brown II* in May, ordering that desegregation occur with "all deliberate speed."

INTRODUCTION

Brown v. Board of Education: An Unfinished Agenda

TAVIS SMILEY

In the spring of 1954, while the Supreme Court was drafting the *Brown* decision, President Eisenhower invited Chief Justice Earl Warren to a White House dinner. After dinner, as the president and the justice strolled arm in arm from the table, Eisenhower said to Warren, "These are not bad people. All they are concerned about is to see that their sweet little girls are not required to sit in school alongside some big overgrown Negroes."[1]

The "people" of whom Eisenhower spoke were the southern segregationists. In fact, John Davis, one of the lawyers for the segregation states in the *Brown* case, was also present at the meal and was seated "within speaking distance"[2] of Justice Warren. Why did Warren report the unflattering presidential remark in his memoirs? He might have done so to support his argument that America's "racial problems" were exacerbated by Eisenhower's failure to have a presidential conversation with the American people about the evils of legal segregation and the correctness of the *Brown* opinion. Warren complained that Eisenhower "never stated that he thought the Decision was right until after he had left the White House."[3]

There is room to quarrel with Warren about whether Eisenhower could have made a useful contribution to the national conversation about *Brown*. This volume amply demonstrates that the president's hostility to racial justice belies his avuncular image in the national mythology.

However, I believe passionately that there exists now, as in the 1950s, a critical need to foster national dialogue about *Brown* and its unfinished agenda. Some serious questions warrant discussion. What is the historical importance of this decision as we look back at the turn of the twenty-first century? Was the racial injustice that the opinion decried reduced as a result of the ruling? Have any of the criticisms of the decision withstood the test of time, and most important, where do we go from here?

This volume is both the starting point for the fiftieth anniversary episode of that *Brown* conversation and a primer for *anyone* who lacks the confidence or information to participate fully in this dialogue. I emphasize "anyone" because the legacy of *Brown* is too vital to be left exclusively to notable legal scholars like the ones who have contributed to this volume. The breadth of this conversation should reflect both a diversity of participants and an appreciation of the international significance of *Brown*. I believe that is why the editors have also included contributions from psychologists, educators, a linguist, an archivist, a journalist, a daughter of a *Brown* plaintiff, as well as voices from the Asian American and Mexican American communities. This is also why they invited me, a political commentator, to write the introduction. All of us share a commitment to making the *Brown* conversation as broad as possible. I hope that this conversation will indeed touch on the implication of *Brown's* principles for the entire human race.

It has been increasingly observed in the scholarly community,[4] but less noted by nonspecialists, that the *Brown* decision is best understood by examining its Cold War context. During the first decade of the Cold War the United States was under enormous pressure from nonwhite nations to demonstrate a commitment to racial equality. The Justice Department's amicus briefs in *Brown* made U.S. foreign policy concerns clear: "It is in the context of the present world struggle between freedom and tyranny that the problem of race discrimination must be viewed. . . . Racial discrimination furnishes grist for the Communist propaganda mills, and it raises doubts even among friendly nations as to the intensity of our devotion to the democratic faith."[5]

The U.S. foreign policy establishment was so pleased with the decision that the Voice of America was broadcasting excerpts hours after it was handed down.[6]

As preparation for the conversation's international spectrum, readers of this volume should take advantage of the chance to eavesdrop on yet another insightful "dialogue" from Professor Derrick Bell, this one based on the counterfactual assumption that the plaintiffs lost the *Brown* case. Bell focuses his analysis on domestic implications. However, take a moment to embrace Bell's imaginative assumption and apply it internationally. Imagine the Soviet Union, armed from the 1950s with the ability to beam propaganda about a U.S. refusal to reject Jim Crow education as a matter of law to the colored peoples of the world! The result might have been a change in Cold War alignments and the prolonging of that costly rivalry.

Imagine further how the leaders of South Africa's apartheid regime would have been emboldened by the plaintiff's loss since they were the only international voices that criticized the real *Brown* decision. Reagan-era advocates of "constructive engagement" with South Africa who attempted to undermine the international boycott would have been even more brazen in their opposition and might very well have prolonged the African National Congress's struggle.

Even in the current world the notions of educational equality that underlie *Brown* resonate beyond our shores. The drafters of a new constitution in U.S.-occupied Iraq will certainly confront the challenge of providing equal educational opportunities in a country with rich ethnic and religious diversity compounded by mutual distrust.

As we broaden our conversation to explore the international context, we must also deepen our appreciation of the domestic backdrop of the decision. The *Brown* opinion was rendered at a time when terror was still a vital weapon in Jim Crow's arsenal. Kahlil Chism's contribution to this volume reminds us that Reverend J. A. DeLaine was shot at, had his church burned, and was ultimately run out of Clarendon County, South Carolina, for soliciting signatures for a petition for *Briggs,* one of the companion cases to *Brown.* Calculated political violence against innocent black civilians was a necessary part of the machinery of white supremacy and was employed to try to derail the fight for desegregation in education. American exposure to terror did not begin on September 11, 2001.

As Paul Robeson noted in early 1955, opponents of the decision were far from satisfied and "responded with howls of anguish and threats of retaliation."[7] Some in the Negro press even argued that the heated opposition to *Brown* in the Deep South fanned the flames of racial hatred and contributed, in Mississippi, to the environment that hatched the lynching of Emmett Till in 1955.[8] If this seems farfetched we should note the disturbing sexual subtext of Eisenhower's comment to Earl Warren, which expresses fear of the proximity of "big overgrown Negroes" to "sweet little [white] girls" and hints at the emotionally volatile core of opposition to desegregation in education.

The conversation in this volume begins with some not so subtle reminders of the conditions of Jim Crow education. Inferior buildings, outmoded secondhand texts, underpaid teachers, and a stigma of inferiority characterized the day-to-day reality of education prior to *Brown.* On the other hand, as a number of contributors point out, behind those Jim Crow walls an amazing process took place in which thousands of blacks were educated in a nurturing environment, with the support of an ingenious, resourceful, largely black, educational community. A number of the articles in this volume suggest that we have not yet devised a calculus sophisticated enough to accurately assess all the gains and losses to black educational life that flowed from *Brown.*

Before we leap into this intriguing book, I want to briefly comment on the historical significance of *Brown* and how important the decision is in the context of our nation's life. We should not ignore the pointed criticisms of *Brown* articulated in these pages, and mine is just the view of one black citizen fortunate enough to be allowed to help moderate this conversation. I am grateful to my friend and noted legal thinker

Raymond M. Brown for the many discussions over the years that have helped to shape my viewpoint.

I stand with the late Judge A. Leon Higginbotham in believing that *Brown,* with all its flaws, stands as the "most important governmental act of any kind since the emancipation proclamation."[9] That said, I will echo a phrase from Cheryl Brown Henderson, the daughter of Plaintiff Oliver Brown: let us "attack the silence."

1

A DOCUMENTARY HISTORY OF *BROWN*

Using Primary Records to Understand *Brown et al. v. Board of Education of Topeka et al.*

KAHLIL G. CHISM

M ay 17, 2004, marked the fiftieth anniversary of the Supreme Court's milestone decision in the *Brown v. Board of Education of Topeka* case. Named after Oliver Brown, the first plaintiff listed in the case, *Brown v. Board of Education* was actually five separate cases, with dozens of plaintiffs, consolidated under a single name, all dealing with racial segregation in public education. The *Brown* decision was a watershed in U.S. legal and civil rights history because it overturned the "separate but equal" doctrine first articulated in the *Plessy v. Ferguson* decision of 1896.[1] By overturning *Plessy,* the Supreme Court ended America's fifty-eight-year-long practice of legal racial segregation in public schools and paved the way for the integration of America's public school systems. Delivering the unanimous opinion of the Court in *Brown,* Chief Justice Earl Warren declared, "In in the field of public education, the doctrine of 'separate but equal' has no place."[2] According to the Court, due to the decision in *Plessy,* "the plaintiffs and others similarly situated" had been

Fourteenth Amendment to the Constitution

"deprived of the equal protection of the laws guaranteed by the Fourteenth Amendment."[3] Although the Court's decision clearly stated *why* segregated public schools were illegal, it did not spell out exactly when and how the states were to begin desegregation. The Court handed down its implementation decree in the spring of 1955, in the decision known as *Brown II*.[4]

On May 31, 1955, Chief Justice Warren delivered the Court's unanimous opinion in *Brown II*. While many praised the Supreme Court for having the wisdom and courage to overturn *Plessy,* those concerned with social justice criticized the Court for weakening the *Brown II* implementation decree by including the ambivalent phrase "with all deliberate speed."[5] Unlike the *Brown* opinion, *Brown II* contained ambiguous phrasing, even though it was intended to instruct the states on how to dismantle segregation in public education. The Court prefaced its plan by acknowledging "the complexities arising from the transition to a system of public education freed of racial discrimination"[6] and seemed to be anticipating, if not inviting, state defiance by using equivocal phrases throughout. The Court called for "admission [of African American students] to public schools *as soon as practicable*" but advised the lower courts that while trying to eliminate obstacles to desegregation they "may properly take into account *the public interest.*" The Supreme Court also asked the lower courts to require the defendants to "make a *prompt and reasonable start toward* full compliance" and advised them that "once such a start has been made, the courts *may find that additional time is necessary.*"[7] It is no wonder, then, that of the seventeen states (and the District of Columbia) where law required segregation in public education, many either stalled or openly defied the Court's ruling. More than a decade after the Court handed down its opinion in *Brown v. Board of Education,* there was practically no change in the racial makeup of black and white southern schools.[8]

While the legal elements of the five cases that make up the *Brown v. Board of Education* decision are well documented, the primary record is unable to convey the numerous stories of personal and social struggles that led up to the decision. Serving as a juncture in U.S. history, the *Brown* decision can be viewed as the inevitable fulfillment of an American promise of freedom, justice, and equality for all of its citizens. *Brown* was a hard-won milestone in the ongoing African American history of grassroots struggle to make America live up to its ideals, a launching pad for the civil rights movement of the 1950s and 1960s, and a textbook example of judicial activism. Unfortunately, the official court records maintained by the National Archives and Records Administration rarely provide insight into the lives of the plaintiffs (most of them children) who actually originated each of the cases or the communities from which they came. The primary records maintained by the National Archives also do not reveal many of the less obvious consequences of the *Brown* decision, such as the loss of a community-based, unique African American pedagogy; the psychological impact of integration on black children; the demographic and economic impact of the decision on the cadre of black educators; or the decision's implications for present-day public education. What the record does provide, however, is insight into the legal chain of events that led to the decision.

In the 1857 case *Dred Scott v. Sandford*,[9] the Supreme Court held that blacks, enslaved or free, could not be citizens of the United States. When he was enslaved to John Sandford in 1846, Dred Scott filed suit against Sandford in St. Louis, Missouri. Scott claimed a right to freedom based on particular circumstances. Scott's previous owner, John Emerson, had taken Scott with him on business to the states of Illinois and Wisconsin from 1834 to 1838, and both of those states had been free states since the Missouri Compromise of 1820. Scott claimed, therefore, that since he had resided in free states for an extended period of time, his owner at the time he filed suit, John Sandford, had no right to hold him as property.[10] Chief Justice Roger Taney, arguing from his interpretation of the original intentions of the framers of the 1787 Constitution, stated in his opinion that at the time of the adoption of the Constitution white society considered blacks a subordinate and inferior class of beings, "with no rights which the White man was bound to respect."[11] Although this decision denied citizenship to blacks, just eight years after *Dred Scott* black people began the long journey toward full citizenship and equal rights through the Emancipation Proclamation; passage and ratification of the Thirteenth, Fourteenth, and Fifteenth Amendments; and the establishment of the Bureau of Refugees, Freedmen, and Abandoned Lands, commonly known as the Freedmen's Bureau.

On March 3, 1865, an act of Congress established the Freedmen's Bureau, whose main mission was to provide services for black people and to help them become self-sufficient in all areas of life. Under the direction of the Freedmen's Bureau, the first black schools were set up to assist freed slaves in their transition from a life of servitude and forced labor to participation in American society, even if only on a highly proscribed level (one of those schools—Howard University—trained and graduated the majority of the legal team that overturned *Plessy*, including Charles Hamilton Houston and Thurgood Marshall). However, in about 1865, southern states began to enact Black Codes to ensure that blacks, educated or not, would never attain social, economic, or political parity with whites.[12] As a result, public schools were segregated, and blacks were barred from serving on juries and testifying against whites. Fortunately, two measures counterbalanced the negative effects of the

Black Codes during the mid-1860s: the passage of the Civil Rights Act of 1866, and the passage and ratification of the Fourteenth Amendment in 1868.

The Civil Rights Act of 1866 guaranteed blacks basic economic rights to contract, sue, and own property. The intention of the law was to protect the civil rights of all males in the United States—including blacks—and to furnish the means of legal recourse when those rights were violated by giving them the right to sue for personal damages. The Fourteenth Amendment, which overruled *Dred Scott v. Sandford,* declared, "All persons born or naturalized in the United States, and sub-ject to the jurisdiction thereof, are citizens of the United States and of the State wherein they reside" and, with particular relevance to the *Brown* decision, "nor shall any State deprive any person of life, liberty, or prop-erty, without due process of law; nor deny to any person within its juris-diction the equal protection of the laws."[13]

The *Slaughterhouse cases* of 1873, a group of cases seemingly having nothing to do with racial segregation, narrowly defined federal power and weakened the Fourteenth Amendment by asserting that most of the rights of citizens should remain under state control.[14] As a result, states that practiced segregation were able to justify their policies based on the theory that segregation in public school systems was an issue for the states to determine, an argument that was repeatedly upheld until the *Brown v. Board of Education* decision. Although Congress attempted to counterbalance the effect of the *Slaughterhouse* decisions with passage of the Civil Rights Act of 1875, which prohibited discrimination in inns, theaters, and other places of public accommodation (the last federal civil rights act passed until 1957), it was quickly overturned. The Supreme Court decided in the civil rights cases in 1883 that the Civil Rights Act of 1875 violated states' rights. That decision charted a direct course for segregation in public education.

Florida became the first state to enact a statute *requiring* segregation in places of public accommodation. Eight other states followed Florida's lead by 1892. By that time in the nation's history, discrimination against blacks at the state and federal level had become such common practice, and white America's belief in the inferiority of black people was engrained enough, that the Supreme Court was able to codify the anti-black sentiment into law with their ruling in the case *Homer Adolph Plessy, Plaintiff in Error v. J. H. Ferguson, Judge of Section "A" Criminal District Court for the Parish of Orleans.* The *Plessy* decision was largely responsible for the rise of the Jim Crow era beginning in the late 1890s, when the practices of comprehensive racial segregation emerged, and racial separation became entrenched.

Homer Plessy challenged an 1890 Louisiana law that required separate train cars for blacks and whites. The Supreme Court held that "separate but equal" facilities for white and black railroad passengers did not violate the equal protection clause of the Fourteenth Amendment, and *Plessy v. Ferguson* established the "separate but equal" doctrine that became the constitutional justification for segregation. Justice John Marshall Harlan, the lone dissenter in *Plessy,* argued that forced segregation of the races stamped blacks with a badge of inferiority.[15] That same argument became a decisive factor in the *Brown v. Board of Education* decision. "In my opinion, the judgment this day rendered," argued Harlan, "will, in time, prove to be quite as pernicious as the decision made by this tribunal in the *Dred Scott* case."[16]

The Supreme Court, in its *Brown v. Board of Education* opinion, referenced six previous cases that had been heard relative to the "separate but equal" doctrine. The first of those cases was *Cumming v. Board of Education of Richmond County, State of Georgia* in 1899.[17] In *Cumming* the Court upheld a local school board's decision to close a black public school due to fiscal constraints, despite the fact that the district continued to operate two white public schools. The opinion stated that there was no evidence in the record that the decision was based on racial discrimination and that the distribution of public funds for public education was within the discretion of school authorities.[18] The *Gong Lum v. Rice* case of 1927 was another case in which the Court applied the "separate but equal" formulation of *Plessy v. Ferguson* to public schools. In this case the Supreme Court held that a Mississippi school district could require a Chinese American girl to attend a segregated black school rather than a white school.[19]

Just eight years after the *Gong Lum* decision, there was a development that would decisively change the course of the legal tide in favor of the eventual overturning of the *Plessy* decision. By 1935 Charles Hamilton Houston set his heart and legal mind to the task of challenging segregation in public education through legal action, all the way to the nation's highest courts.

In 1935 Charles Houston, then head of the National Association for the Advancement of Colored People (NAACP), with the assistance of his protégé and former student in the Howard University School of Law, Thurgood Marshall, began challenging segregation in graduate and professional schools. Houston's rationale for attacking segregated law schools was two-pronged. First, he believed the establishment of "separate but equal" law school facilities for black and white students would be too costly for the states to achieve and maintain. Second, he was counting on the fact that white judges who matriculated in some of the nation's finest law schools could not, in good conscience, suggest that black lawyers in segregated schools received legal education "equal" to their own. The question of whether states were actually able to establish black law schools equal to their white counterparts would repeatedly surface over the next decade, beginning with the case *State of Missouri ex. rel. Gaines v. Canada* in 1938.

In *Gaines v. Canada*, the Supreme Court decided in favor of Lloyd Gaines, a black student who had been refused admission to the University of Missouri Law School. This case set a precedent for other states to attempt to "equalize" black school facilities rather than integrate them. The Court held that the state must furnish Gaines "within its borders facilities for legal education substantially equal to those which the State there afforded for persons of the White race, whether or not other Negroes sought the same opportunity."[20] Correctly foreseeing that many states might try equalization rather than desegregation, the NAACP defense team attacked the "equal" standard so that the "separate" standard would, in turn, become vulnerable. Therefore, in 1948 the NAACP Board of Directors formally endorsed Thurgood Marshall's view that the NAACP should devote its efforts to an all-out attack on segregation in public education, rather than pressing for the equalization of segregated facilities.

The year 1949 was another pivotal year in the long struggle against segregation. In the fall, Thurgood Marshall and other NAACP officials met with black residents of Clarendon County, South Carolina. They agreed that the NAACP would launch a test case against segregation in public schools if at least twenty plaintiffs could be found. By November, Harry Briggs and nineteen other plaintiffs were assembled, and the NAACP filed a class action lawsuit against the Clarendon County School Board in the case *Harry Briggs et al. v. R. W. Elliott et al.* The *Briggs* case featured the social science testimony and the doll study of Dr. Kenneth Clark and became one of the cases consolidated by the Supreme Court into *Brown v. Board of Education.*[21]

VOICES OF THE ERA

Emanuel Richardson is the son of Lucrisher Richardson, one of twenty plaintiffs in *Harry Briggs et al. v. R. W. Elliott et al.*

In 1951 the Clarendon County, South Carolina, government spent, on average, $44.32 annually to educate a black child and $166.45 per white child. Black children paid for their school materials (i.e., in addition to the taxes they paid) while white children did not incur this expense.

With motivation from Reverand J. A. DeLaine, a pastor in Clarendon County, twenty of the county's black parents filed *Briggs v. Elliott.* DeLaine was instrumental in getting this case to the Supreme Court. A warrant was issued for his arrest after he defended himself against shots fired into his home by white protesters. His church and his home were burned to the ground, and he was eventually run out of town by tremendous threats to his family. He was never able to return to South Carolina because the state refused to cancel the warrant for his arrest until several years after his death.

At the time of the Briggs decision in 1954, I was eleven and didn't realize what it meant. My mother came to me and said that they had this petition going around and everybody in the neighborhood was going to sign it. Our church on Historic Liberty Hill is where they decided they would all sign and suffer the consequences regardless.

We lived on a white man's land. We rented. One day, Mr. Anderson, the cotton gin owner, came to our house to speak to my dad. He had found out that they circulated a petition to integrate the schools. He told my father that the whites were willing to do other things like build new schools to offer separate but equal. My mom came outside and told him that if he was going to put the family off the land, then he would just have to go ahead and do it because she was going to sign the petition anyway.

All of the petitioners felt the same way, Mr. Briggs, Barry Oliver, the Parsons, and the Richards, of course, were some of the champions of that movement. I was just eleven so I didn't really have the sense of what was actually happening, but I knew what we had to do and I knew it was important that we do it.

Our parents were tired of the discrimination, the inadequate training for our young people, and the inadequate books. We were getting hand-me-down books; when an edition would expire, they would pass it on to the black schools. We were

Emanuel Richardson

always two or three editions behind. We had to walk about two miles to school while the whites would get on the bus and taunt us and call us names. We just got a little bit fed up with all of it. Times were changing. Thurgood Marshall started coming down to South Carolina to meet with all of the pastors. Reverend DeLaine was at the forefront. They all just realized that they needed to do this for the betterment of our black race.

By 1950 the legal tide appeared to turn favorably for those who longed to see the dismantling of segregation in public education. In that year Charles Houston took on one of his last cases, *Bolling v. Sharpe.* The *Sharpe* case turned out to be the first of the five cases eventually bundled and heard by the Supreme Court as *Brown v. Board of Education.* The Supreme Court also handed down significant rulings in two other cases that year: *Sweatt v. Painter* and *McLaurin v. Oklahoma State Regents.* In the *Sweatt* case the Court held that the University of Texas Law School must admit a black student, Herman Sweatt. The University of Texas Law School was far superior in its offerings and resources to the separate black law school that had been hastily established in a downtown basement. The Court held that Texas, therefore, had failed to provide separate but equal education. In *McLaurin,* the Court invalidated the University of Oklahoma's requirement that George McLaurin, a black student admitted to a graduate program unavailable to him at the state's black school, sit in separate sections of, or in spaces adjacent to, the classroom, the library, and the cafeteria. The Court held that these restrictions were unconstitutional because they interfered with his "ability to study, to engage in discussions, and exchange views with other students, and, in general, to learn his profession."[22] That was a significant turning point in the argument against segregation because it was the first time a court acknowledged that equality of education was based on more than merely the physical facilities. Although Charles Hamilton Houston died in 1950, it was not before he had a chance to witness the beginnings of change in the future of American public education due to his legal strategy.

By 1951 the momentum of the NAACP legal team had increased dramatically, and they were filing cases challenging segregation in various parts of the country. In February, members of the legal team filed *Brown v. Board of Education of Topeka.* Spottswood Robinson, a former dean of the Howard University School of Law, filed a challenge to Virginia's segregated schools in May. The *Davis v. Prince Edward County, Virginia,* and *Briggs v. Elliott* cases went to trial that same month.[23] In October NAACP attorneys Louis Redding and Jack Greenberg were cocounsel for two very closely related Delaware cases that went to trial that year, *Gebhart v. Belton* and *Gebhart v. Bulah.*[24] By June, Robert

Carter was leading the NAACP into the first trial phase of the *Brown v. Board of Education of Topeka* case.

When the *Briggs* case went to trial in Clarendon County, South Carolina, Thurgood Marshall and the NAACP legal team presented a vast array of social science evidence showing how segregation harmed black schoolchildren, including evidence from sociologist Kenneth Clark's controversial doll study. The U.S. Court of Appeals for the Fourth Circuit denied the *Briggs* plaintiffs' request to order desegregation of the Clarendon County schools and instead ordered the equalization of black schools. Judge Justin Waring, as the lone dissenter, supporting the disappointed plaintiffs, wrote, "From their testimony, it was clearly apparent, as it should be to any thoughtful person, irrespective of having such expert testimony, that segregation in education can never produce equality and that it is an evil that must be eradicated."[25]

In August a three-judge panel, ruling with regard to the question of the equality of physical plants, unanimously held in the *Brown v. Board of Education* case that no willful, intentional, or substantial discrimination existed in Topeka's schools. The panel found that the physical facilities in white and black schools were comparable and that the Supreme Court's decisions in *Sweatt v. Painter* and *McLaurin* only applied to graduate education.

In March 1952, a three-judge U.S. District Court in Richmond, Virginia, found in favor of the School Board of Prince Edward County, Virginia, in the *Davis* case. Under the doctrine of "separate but equal," the court unanimously rejected the *Davis* plaintiffs' request to order desegregation of Prince Edward County schools, ordering the "equalization" of black schools instead. In April a Delaware court ruled that the plaintiffs in both *Gebhart* cases were being denied equal protection of the laws and that they were entitled to immediate admission to the local white public school. This decision did not, however, strike down the segregation laws of the state of Delaware, and the state Board of Education appealed the decision.

The Supreme Court announced in June that it would hear oral arguments in *Briggs* and *Brown* during the upcoming October 1952 term. Finally, in October 1952, just days before arguments were to be heard in

Briggs and *Brown,* the Supreme Court announced a postponement. Three weeks later, the Court said that it would also hear the Delaware cases, as well as *Davis v. Prince Edward County, Virginia,* and the District of Columbia case, *Bolling et al. v. Sharpe et al.* The Supreme Court agreed to hear all five of the school desegregation cases collectively. This grouping was significant because it showed that school segregation was a national issue, not just a southern one. The moment that the plaintiffs, the NAACP legal team, and innumerable African Americans and other people of conscience had been working toward finally arrived on December 9, 10, and 11, when the Court held the first round of arguments in the five cases, officially bundled together as *Brown v. Board of Education.*

In September 1953 Chief Justice Fred Vinson Jr. died unexpectedly of a heart attack, and President Eisenhower nominated California governor Earl Warren, as interim chief justice. Because of Vinson's concerns about the possibility of racial unrest if desegregation were ordered, his previous rulings in cases regarding segregation, and his perception of the problem as "essentially political and social in nature, not legal," many believed that Vinson, from Kentucky, would not have ruled against segregation.[26] President Eisenhower chose Warren not only because he felt that Warren would take a moderate approach to the case, but also because he was sixty-two years old. Eisenhower wanted a younger justice on the Court, someone who would be there for a while. History revealed that Eisenhower was surprised by just how liberal the Warren Court became.

A second round of arguments in the *Brown* case was held in December 1953. In March 1954, the Senate confirmed Earl Warren's appointment as chief justice.

Finally, on May 17, 1954, the Supreme Court handed down their decision in the *Brown* case and ruled that state-sanctioned segregation of public schools was a violation of the Fourteenth Amendment and was, therefore, unconstitutional. The Court rendered a separate opinion on *Bolling v. Sharpe* because the Fourteenth Amendment to the U.S. Constitution was not applicable in the District of Columbia.

After the decision, the District of Columbia and some school districts

in the border states began to desegregate their schools voluntarily. However, state legislatures in Alabama, Georgia, Mississippi, South Carolina,
and Virginia adopted resolutions of "interposition and nullification" that
declared the Court's decision to be "null, void, and [of] no effect."[27]

In another twist of fate, Associate Justice Robert H. Jackson died
suddenly in October 1954, forcing the president to nominate yet another
justice. President Eisenhower nominated John Marshall Harlan, the
grandson of the lone dissenter in *Plessy*, to fill the vacancy. After extensive hearings before the Senate, Harlan was sworn in as an associate justice in March 1955, just two months before the Court handed down its
opinion in *Brown II*, ordering that desegregation occur with "all deliberate speed."

VOICES OF THE ERA

Elizabeth Briscoe Wilson is the university librarian at Lincoln University in
Jefferson City, Missouri. A native of Missouri, she has been active in archiving African American history in the Midwest. She is a historical interpreter
and is one the few college librarians who have taken a leadership role in
reorganizing and archiving documents from the *Brown* legacy.

> *The Historically Black Colleges and University (HBCU) archives
> hold a treasure trove of information. Some of the documents and
> resources we have are only in our archives—for instance, this
> scrapbook is dedicated to the Brown case and on integration. It
> was likely constructed by a library assistant working at Lincoln Uni-
> versity and, although not an archivist, he or she held on to some
> important history. That person cut and clipped all sorts of infor-
> mation. It is not on archival paper, nor has it been enclosed for
> preservation, and it is only by the grace of God that we still have
> it available to us. We used to be in a building that had leaks, did
> not have air conditioning, and often did not have heat. Uncon-
> trolled temperature is the worst enemy of archives. I don't know*

how much longer we will be able to preserve items like this unless we have trained archivists to help us.

More than one hundred HBCUs are still open, operating, and active, but very little money has been set aside to help us with the kind of archival restoration work that is needed. We also need to scan and digitize the information so we can make these documents available on the Web for those who cannot come to our archives. There is information here that we have access to that no one else knows about.

The Lincoln University archive is the first in the school's 150-year history. We have formed an association with Hampton University and North Carolina A&T called the 1890 Library Initiative, an attempt to preserve our important documents and make them accessible to the public. If we lose this history at the HBCUs, we will have lost much of the history of the experience of African American people whose efforts were vital to the building of America. We have to ensure that history continues to be studied. The National Archives needs to work with the HBCU librarians to keep this kind of information available for scholars and for posterity.

Elizabeth Briscoe Wilson

The documentary record of the *Brown v. Board of Education* case includes reply briefs for appellants and respondents; acknowledgments of receipts of service; supplemental briefs; judgments; orders; statistical charts of population and race; lists of related cases and statutes; transcripts of court records; proceedings and testimony for the U.S. District Court, Kansas; petitions for appeal; motions of various state attorneys general and organizations for permission to file briefs; resolutions from state legislatures regarding segregation in public schools; and mandate letters.

Accessioned by the National Archives in 1977, documents from all five cases can be found on microfilm at the National Archives' College Park, Maryland, facility, as well as our facilities in East Point, Georgia; Center City, Philadelphia, Pennsylvania; and the National Archives Central Plains Regional Center, Kansas City, Missouri.[28] Primary source materials also can be found in the U.S. Supreme Court library, in the Manuscript Division of the Library of Congress, in the case files of the NAACP Legal Defense Fund, and in the law school library holdings of various universities.

Many historians continue to preserve the oral history and legacy of the individual activists who and the communities that were at the heart of all of the cases, big and small, that led to the *Brown v. Board of Education* decision. A comprehensive familiarity with the documentary record serves as a foundation for appreciating why the best intentions of the *Brown* decision—full integration and equal access to quality education for African Americans enrolled in the nation's public schools—remain only partially accomplished, even today.[29]

2

THE ATTORNEYS

Paragons or Parasites?

Some younger readers of this volume, and I hope there are many, may hear the name Thurgood Marshall and think of the pithy comment he made at his televised retirement press conference. When asked whether his successor on the Supreme Court should be black or white, the African American justice replied, "A black snake is just as dangerous as a white one."

Other readers will recall Marshall's role as an architect and principal advocate in *Brown.* Juan Williams vividly describes that role and just as important introduces (or reprises for us) the roles of other committed lawyers in *Brown* and its companion cases. In acknowledging the impact of Charles Hamilton Houston, a legendary legal activist and mentor to Marshall and others, Williams resurrects for lawyers, would be lawyers, as well as those who care about the law, the challenge of Houston's belief that a lawyer who is not a social engineer is a "parasite."

—Tavis Smiley

Attorneys celebrating the *Brown v. Board of Education* decision.

Never-Ending Argument

JUAN WILLIAMS

Fifty years ago, when Thurgood Marshall argued before the U.S. Supreme Court for an end to segregated schools, he made a simple case for simple justice. At six feet, three inches tall, Marshall was a big, chain-smoking man in his mid-forties who smiled even as he presented the case before the Supreme Court. Thurgood Marshall was committed to fighting segregated schools because he knew their consequences firsthand. When Marshall was born in 1908, black schools, without exception, had far fewer resources than rival white schools. The black teachers in the black schools were paid less than the white teachers in the white schools, and a diploma from the black schools was viewed as second-rate.

When Marshall stood before the Court to insist on a black child's right to attend any public school, he equated quality schools with integrated schools because the whites-only schools always had the best facilities and resources. He watched his own mother teach kindergarten in the second-rate facilities available to black children in a segregated public school system; he went to those colored schools in Baltimore City. He then attended a college founded to serve young black people excluded from white public schools by the laws of segregation. And when he looked for a law school, he found that his state's major law school, the University of Maryland's law school, did not accept people of color. As a result, Marshall went to Howard University School of Law, a school founded to educate former slaves excluded on the basis of race from every other law school in the land.

That personal history of exclusion did not stop Marshall from getting an education. It made it harder for him, a middle-class black child, to get a good education. And he saw that in many areas of the nation it was nearly impossible for any black child, but especially a poor black student, to get the education necessary to compete in American society. Most black children of that era did not choose inferior schools. They did not choose all-black schools. They simply found themselves living in a world where their educational prospects were limited by their skin color; people of color were forced into separate and inferior classrooms. They either scrambled for a place in the few black schools or went into the world without an education.

Speaking with the slight southern drawl of a kid from Baltimore, Marshall told the Court that when Congress approved the Fourteenth Amendment to the Constitution—guaranteeing all citizens equal rights—it outlawed segregation. That meant, he argued, that Congress opened the doors to the nation's public schools for America's children, black and white.

Marshall's simple argument brought a simple rebuttal from the lawyer on the other side, a man with a childhood full of segregationist memories from his native South Carolina. John W. Davis was the dean of American lawyers in the middle of the twentieth century. At the time, the silver-haired Davis had argued more cases before the Supreme Court than any other living lawyer. He had been solicitor general, the federal government's top lawyer before the high Court, and once reigned as president of the American Bar Association. Davis also had been the Democrats' presidential candidate in 1924. That stature and Davis's friendship with many of the justices on the Court led the segregationist governor of South Carolina, James Byrnes—who was a former U.S. Supreme Court justice—to personally ask Davis to argue the case before the Supreme Court.

The aristocratic Davis, approaching eighty at the time of the *Brown* case, confidently told the Court that the historical record showed Congress never intended to end school segregation when it passed the Fourteenth Amendment in 1868. The proof, he said, pointing out the obvious, was that Congress never acted to end segregated schools even after it passed the law. In fact, Congress had created a segregated public school system in the nation's capital, Washington, D.C., in 1871, three years after the Fourteenth Amendment was law.

Davis posed a question for the nine white men on the Supreme Court. Speaking with a patronizing concern for black children, Davis asked: Why should black children be taken from all-black schools, where they are "happy and inspired," and be forced to attend integrated schools, where they will be "ridiculed and hated"? Davis contended that segregated schools were equal in the sense that they offered an appropriate education for blacks. Integrated schools, he predicted, meant the destruction of those nurturing, all-black schools for the descendants of uneducated slaves. Davis used one of Aesop's fables to make his point: "The dog with a fine piece of meat in his mouth crossed a bridge and saw the [reflection of the meat] in the stream and plunged for it and lost both shadow and substance."

That day in court, when Marshall and Davis faced off, came about because of a collective effort that had begun more than twenty years earlier. The spark that started the fire was Charles Hamilton Houston's vision of dismantling *Plessy v. Ferguson*. Thurgood Marshall succeeded Houston as the NAACP's special counsel, and continued to implement the legal campaign Houston had developed years before. Marshall successfully carried the torch Houston had lit for so many of his former Howard University School of Law students who comprised the NAACP Legal Defense Fund, Inc., team.

The NAACP had, in the 1930s, commissioned lawyer Nathan Margold to develop a strategy to positively affect the legal status of blacks in the United States. The Margold Report argued that under segregation the facilities provided for blacks would never be equal to those maintained for whites. As such, this was a violation of the "separate but equal" principle in *Plessy*. Margold proposed a series of lawsuits that would challenge the system. Houston agreed that Margold's suggestion could serve as a blueprint for the NAACP's battle, but he advocated gradual challenge and reliance on legal precedent. Houston's war plan for the NAACP focused on litigating planned test cases across the country to generate favorable legal precedents, to lay the foundation for an eventual all-out attack on racial discrimination and segregation. The cases were to have a "sharply defined legal issue" that could be "supported by demonstrable evidence." Houston focused on three primary goals: unequal pay for black teachers, unequal transportation for black students, and the inequality of graduate study programs for black students at state-supported segregated institutions. This third focus was the most precedent-generating, prompting three Supreme Court cases, *Gaines v. Canada, McLaurin v. Oklahoma State Regents,* and *Sweatt v. Painter,* which eventually paved the way to topple *Plessy* with the *Brown* decision.

The campaign against *Plessy* would find many of its legal soldiers at Howard University Law School. Houston had already begun to transform the School of Law as its first black dean, quickly upgrading the faculty, reorganizing the curriculum, and improving the library. Houston led the school's successful efforts to attain accreditation by the Association of American Law Schools and the American Bar Association. He shaped the school into a significant institution, at the time training almost a quarter of the nation's black law students, including Thurgood Marshall. Houston impressed upon his students that they were to serve their community as social engineers, arguing that each was to be a "mouthpiece for the weak and a sentinel guarding against wrong" who must "use the law as an instrument available to [the] minority unable to adopt direct action to achieve its place in the community and nation."[1] According to Houston, any lawyer who failed to do so was a parasite on society.

VOICES OF THE ERA

Oliver Hill is a 1933 Howard University graduate. He attended Howard's School of Law with Thurgood Marshall, where they both graduated with honors. Hill became the NAACP's contact in Virginia and was part of Charles Hamilton Houston's team of lawyers strategically working to dismantle segregation in public education. Mr. Hill recently retired from his practice with Hill, Tucker, and Marsh. Still an activist in his nineties, on January 7, 2003, he was instrumental in the Virginia legislature's acknowledgment that "massive resistance" as its response to the *Brown* decision was wrong.

> *Reading the Constitution is what made me want to go to law school. My stepfather's brother was a lawyer who went to Howard University School of Law. After he died in about 1927, his widow*

gave me an annotated code of the Constitution of the United States. The annotated version included the leading cases and provided interpretations of the varying provisions. It was obvious to me after reading the Fourteenth Amendment that segregation laws were in violation of the Constitution. We had no chance of getting any rights at all in the late twenties. You couldn't even get a law enacted in Congress to make lynching a crime, much less do anything about giving us political or economic rights. It seemed to me that the only way we would be able to get over this hurdle was through the courts.

Dr. Mordecai Johnson, president of Howard University, was determined to make Howard's School of Law first-class. He put Charles Hamilton Houston in charge of carrying out this mission. Charlie attracted some great lawyers and great students. From the time of its inception in 1867 until 1930, the law school was an evening school with adjunct professors who were mostly judges or lawyers. But Charlie was determined to turn it into a full-time law school and earn accreditation. He worked so hard that we were able to earn accreditation in one year.

Charles Houston was a real mentor. Charlie's philosophy was that "any lawyer who wasn't a social engineer was a parasite on society." He drilled that concept into my head. I came to understand that you either try to improve conditions in the society in which you live or else you're just a drag on society altogether. We were always studying precedent and trying to figure out ways and approaches to challenge segregation. We thought about segregation all the time. Dismantling it was our aim.

Charlie developed our legal strategy. We would challenge the law as it existed, the notion of separate but equal. Nothing was equal. For example, in Richmond in 1940, the beginning salary for Negro teachers was somewhere around $350 to $399. The highest salary was $999 after many years of service. The beginning salary for white teachers was $1,000 and went up to $1,700 or $1,800. We challenged this kind of disparity and others, including that the whites were riding buses to school and the Negroes were walking.

I filed suit in Sussex County because Negroes had to pay for their children to go to school by bus. We were arguing for them to make it equal, recognizing that there was no way to make two school systems equal. To say they could provide equal school systems was out of the question. Charlie also figured we could educate judges, whites, and other Negroes. But there were a lot of us who didn't want to rock the boat, people who were afraid of losing their jobs.

After Charlie filed suits, he would go to the editors of the papers to talk about his views on separate but equal. Initially we had some white support and even a little bit of support from the newspapers. A lot of white people thought Negroes ought to have equality. They didn't want to associate with us, they didn't believe in interracial marriages, but as far as riding buses, streetcars, going to theaters, or restaurants, whites didn't object to us doing these things so long as Negroes and whites were separate.

After some time, we made progress. We thought we had finally convinced and educated the Supreme Court judges with the Sweatt v. Painter law school case in Texas. You can imagine what a one-student law school amounted to. It was ridiculous. No library, no prestige, no association with fellow students, nothing. After hearing Judge Vinson's favorable decision in 1950, we thought the Supreme Court had come around, so we began to challenge segregation in every city.

I think we were right in how we went about fighting against segregation, although we didn't anticipate that much opposition to desegregating the schools. Segregation went deeper and wider than we thought. When Vinson wrote the decision in the Sweatt case we really believed we had him on our side. Now we know he never was on our side. For him, providing improvements, equality, or opportunity was a separate issue from Negro children going to school with white children.

Warren's appointment really was the best thing that ever happened to us. Eisenhower clearly wasn't aware of Warren's position on segregation because Eisenhower was a segregationist himself. Although the Supreme Court found the laws unconstitutional, they didn't provide a mandate to do anything about them. They were still trying to find some way to appease the South. The purpose of Brown II was to find a remedy. Frankfurter convinced Warren to add the line "all deliberate speed." That was supposed to sort of give them time, and the school boards took advantage of it. This made it possible for each state to find ways of avoiding doing what they were supposed to do. There was only one way to ever make the states do right, and that was to demand that they do right.

I filed suit in Warren County, Virginia, and the court ordered the school board to equalize their facilities. Former governor Battle called me one day to say that he was representing the school board and that he needed some more time. He wanted thirty more days in addition to the twenty-one days the court provided. It didn't make any sense to me, I really didn't think it would make a difference whether I agreed to more time or not. We went to court over the issue. I was surprised when the judge did not support their request; he ordered the school board to desegregate immediately. All they were doing was trying to waste a whole lot of time. They knew it. We knew it.

It is time to start thinking in terms of being humans here on planet Earth. We've got to get over these ideas of being American,

Oliver Hill

Chinese, French, or English. We need to eliminate ethnic bound-
aries and national boundaries. All of us have the same basic
needs—health, food, housing, and opportunities to recreate.
Everyone also needs to have a livelihood, to be able to work in
some capacity. There isn't anything more demoralizing than not
being able to do anything. I'm trying now to get us to have a bet-
ter concept of revolution and recognize that change is inevitable.
We must direct that change in the common interest. We've got to
stop thinking in terms of what will make us rich. We're moving
faster technologically than we are educating people. We're going
to have to replace competition with cooperation.

Houston's legal team was initially comprised of his cousin William
Hastie, Thurgood Marshall, and other NAACP lawyers. Following Houston's framework, the team did not immediately attack *Plessy* but rather
focused on the inequality of facilities that segregation produced. Houston believed that by gradually launching test cases it would eventually
become obvious that separate could never be equal; and since the Constitution required equality, not separation, one would have to be elimi-
nated to assure the other. From 1935 to 1940, Houston oriented the
NAACP's efforts toward graduate-level education, not cases involving
elementary or high schools, predicting that judges would be more likely
to rule favorably. This "equalization strategy" demanded that the facilities provided for black students be made equal to those available to white
students, carefully stopping short of a direct challenge to *Plessy*.

Houston determined that the states that practiced segregation could
not afford to maintain two separate but equal school systems. This thinking was applied in *Murray v. University of Maryland* (1936), which resulted
in the desegregation of the University of Maryland's Law School. *Missouri
ex. rel. Gaines v. Canada* also employed this strategy, and the Court forced
the University of Missouri Law School to admit its first black student. The
Gaines victory was used as a tool to compel southern universities to give
black graduate students the same opportunities that had always been

given to whites. This ruling established the "*Gaines* principle," which mandated that a black student had the right to attend the state's only existing facility if no separate and equal facilities were available.

Following *Gaines,* Houston and his team successfully attacked salary discrimination against black teachers, ended segregation on interstate transit and in the armed forces, and abolished the white primary. The legal team was threatened with physical violence, but they persisted in their efforts to establish precedent in the courts. Gaines paved the way for the *McLaurin v. Oklahoma State Regents* and *Sweatt v. Painter* decisions in 1950.

In *McLaurin,* the Supreme Court held that black students could not be subjected to segregation if it interfered with meaningful classroom instruction and interaction with other students. The practices of making the black student sit in the classroom doorway or at a separate lunch table were deemed violations of the "separate but equal" principle. Most notably in *Sweatt v. Painter,* the Supreme Court ruled that a separate law school established for black students to prevent admission to the all-white University of Texas School of Law could not provide a legal education "equal" to that available to white students.

These sweet NAACP victories were tinged with sorrow, as Houston died in 1950, the very year of these important decisions.

Four years later, as testimony and arguments were given for *Brown,* Charles Hamilton Houston's role as architect and chief strategist for the NAACP was more visible than ever. When the Supreme Court called for evidence showing whether the framers and ratifiers of the Fourteenth Amendment had desegregation of schools in mind when they wrote the amendment in 1868, the Legal Defense Fund staff used the framework engineered by Houston to guide them through their long summer of research in 1953. The Legal Defense Fund staff spent months poring over congressional and state legislative debates, searching for every weakness that reinforced Houston's vision that *Plessy* served as a spur to segregation laws. Legal scholars, historians, and social scientists also were employed to discuss every aspect of the Fourteenth Amendment.

By the time the NAACP Legal Defense Fund, Inc., led by Thurgood Marshall, appeared before the Supreme Court to argue the cases held

NAACP Lawyers Representing the Plaintiffs in Each of the Five Supreme Court Cases

On the briefs were: Robert L. Carter, Thurgood Marshall, Spottswood W. Robinson III, Louis L. Redding, Jack Greenberg, George E. C. Hayes, William R. Ming Jr., Constance Baker Motley, James M. Nabrit Jr., Charles S. Scott, Frank D. Reeves, Harold R. Boulware, Oliver W. Hill, George M. Johnson, Loren Miller, Arthur D. Shores, and A. T. Walden

NAACP Legal Defense Fund counsel included: Charles L. Black Jr., Elwood H. Chisolm, William T. Coleman Jr., Charles T. Duncan, George E. C. Hayes, Loren Miller, William R. Ming Jr., Constance Baker Motley, David E. Pinsky, Frank D. Reeves, John Scott, and Jack B. Weinstein.

collectively as *Brown v. Board,* its task force included more than two hundred members. Among this stellar team were James M. Nabrit Jr., George E. C. Hayes, Robert L. Carter, Charles S. Scott, Harold Boulware, Louis L. Redding, Jack Greenberg, Oliver M. Hill, and Spottswood W. Robinson III.

James M. Nabrit Jr., Howard professor of law and later president of

Howard University, inherited *Bolling v. Sharpe* after Houston's death. Nabrit, working with another Howard law professor, George E. C. Hayes, adapted Houston's strategy to the segregated schools in Washington, D.C. They argued that Congress did not pass any law that forced the District of Columbia to maintain separate schools. Meanwhile, Charles Scott and Robert Carter were two of the attorneys representing the plaintiffs in *Brown v. Board of Topeka.* Charles Scott, along with his brother John, had been the lawyers who filed suit on behalf of the NAACP. Robert Carter worked on the case from NAACP Legal Defense Fund headquarters in New York City.

VOICES OF THE ERA

Charles Scott Jr. is the son of attorney Charles Scott Sr., who argued the original *Brown* case with his brother John Scott. Grandfather Elisha also argued *Webb v. School District No. 90,* known as *Webb v. South Park* in Merriam, Kansas, one of the cases that precipitated the Topeka suit.

The Walker School for black children in Merriam, Kansas, in the late 1940s was an old and dilapidated one-room building. Black parents were outraged by these conditions, especially in comparison to the $90,000 South Park Elementary School, which had been built for white students. When their children were denied admission to the new South Park Elementary School, Webb and other black parents opened a home school with teacher Corinthian Nutter, who taught these children for more than a year.

Elisha Scott took the lead in the *Webb* case. The Kansas Supreme Court ruled in 1949 that equal facilities must be provided for all children, and the Board was forced to admit black children to South Park Elementary School on the basis that the school facilities were unequal.

> *I was not of school age when the* Brown *case was filed, and quite frankly I did not appreciate its meaning until I was twelve or thir-' teen. My grandfather Elisha Scott was the attorney for the case that precipitated* Brown, Webb v. South Park. *South Park is a little*

community just outside Kansas City. In 1948 they built a brand-new state-of-the-art school for the white children, and they acquired a one-room shack for all the black children, who were in grades one through eight. The black school only had two teachers, neither of them certified. I think they were volunteers. The school had outdoor toilets, no indoor plumbing, while just a few blocks away stood the brand-new state-of-the-art school. A number of citizens

Charles Scott

who didn't think this was right contacted my grandfather to bring a suit to gain admission for black students to that new school. My grandfather argued that case before the Kansas Supreme Court. Following that decision, black students were admitted to that school. From that case, the decision to challenge the separate-but-equal doctrine in Kansas and to challenge segregation itself followed.

My grandfather and Thurgood Marshall had quite an association, but my grandfather was an independent person who marched to his own tune. He wasn't known as a general for justice. He was known simply as a foot soldier for justice.

Robert Carter was instrumental in developing the strategy of using the testimony of social scientists and other experts who provided evidence on segregation's devastating effects on the psychological health of black children. Harold Boulware, chief counsel for the South Carolina NAACP, represented the plaintiff in *Briggs v. Elliott* case. Boulware was best known as the lawyer who led the effort to gain equal pay for equal work for black teachers in South Carolina. Louis L. Redding, Delaware's first black lawyer, worked with Jack Greenberg on the *Gebhart* cases. Redding was already well known for defending black students. In 1950 he won *Parker v. University of Delaware*, which forced the University of Delaware to allow black people to study there. Jack Greenberg, who worked with Marshall on cases in Texas and Oklahoma that integrated law schools and graduate schools *(Sweatt v. Painter* and *McLaurin v. Oklahoma State Regents)*, would eventually succeed Marshall to lead the Legal Defense Fund in the 1960s. Oliver M. Hill and his partner Spottswood Robinson III represented the plaintiffs in the *Davis v. Prince Edward County, Virginia,* case. Hill and Robinson once had seventy-five cases pending in court. They were best known for filing more civil rights suits in Virginia than the total filed in all other southern states in the segregation era. The *Washington Post* once estimated that Hill and Robinson were responsible for winning more than $50 million in higher pay, new buses, and better schools for black teachers and students.

The arguments in the *Brown* case took place in two stages. The first set of arguments was made in December 1952; a second round took place before the Court in December 1953. Paul Wilson, the assistant attorney general of Kansas who represented his state at the Supreme Court, later said that despite the many lawyers in the Court, all eyes and ears turned to two men—Davis and Marshall. "The personalities of each seemed peculiarly appropriate to the cause that he represented . . . a duel between the champion of aristocracy and rationalism on the one hand and populism and humanitarianism on the other."

The conflicting views that Marshall and Davis presented in the *Brown* case regarding American history, law, and race relations opened the door to arguments over affirmative action, busing, redistricting, and social justice that are still at the top of the nation's agenda fifty years later.

The contrast between Marshall and Davis went beyond the color of their skin. Marshall, about half Davis's age, was accustomed to speaking to segregationist juries as well as to openly bigoted judges. And Davis was a segregationist. He had written that there are "anatomical differences" and "differences in intellectual processes, in tastes and aptitudes." Davis's suggestion to the Supreme Court that black people were better off in their own schools—which never were equal due to lack of funding—was, in Davis's mind, a virtue. He said it was an opportunity to give special attention to the needs of black children. Blatant disparities in school funding, school facilities, and the quality of education did not bother him.

JOHN W. DAVIS'S THINKING
RESURRECTED

As early as 1967, Clarence Thomas, Marshall's successor on the Supreme Court, previewed the current turn away from integration. Writing in the *Howard University Law Journal*, the future Supreme Court justice wrote that "*Brown* was a missed opportunity, as all of its progeny, whether they involve busing, affirmative action, or redistricting." Thomas, who was then head of the Equal Employment Opportunity Commission, wrote that the Warren Court made a mistake by focusing on the "feeling of inferiority" that segregated schools might produce in black students. Justice Thomas wrote that by making "sensitivity the paramount issue," the Court turned away from principles of equality and liberty for all citizens, as outlined in the Declaration of Independence and the Constitution. Thomas opened a line of argument for Americans that has become popular among whites and blacks. He said that Americans should be free to rise "above petty squabbling over 'quotas,' 'affirmative action,' and 'race-conscious remedies for social ills.'" In other words, Americans should be free to create schools with students of any color as long as they are good schools. Marshall's argument that integration is the key to equal education for all children is losing ground fast in the court of popular opinion.

This is not a case of some modern-day John W. Davis successfully arguing that there is nothing wrong with segregated schools. Rather, people—black, brown, and white—say openly that they are tired of working on busing plans and other strategies for desegregating schools. It is the lack of commitment to work on integrating schools to ensure equal educational opportunity that stands out in this era and that gives new life to John W. Davis's embrace of segregated schools.

The argument for the current reversion to segregation in American education is similar to John W. Davis's argument that minority children may feel more comfortable and accepted in a single-race environment. There is less racial friction, and minority teachers are more nurturing of minority students. But what can't be argued is that segregated schools are the equal of integrated schools when it comes to education. There is no statistical basis for saying that segregated black and Latino schools, even voluntarily segregated schools, are equal in educational quality to majority white schools. That was true when John W. Davis argued the *Brown* case, and it is true today. That failed argument led to his defeat in midcentury, and the same failure betrays efforts to turn away from looking at race in today's increasingly segregated schools.

That is why fifty years after *Brown v. Board* was decided, Thurgood Marshall's argument for integrated schools remains compelling and still defeats John W. Davis's argument.

Marshall did not scream "racism" in response to Davis's argument. He didn't want to risk angering the all-white justices. Arguing before a Court produced by segregationist politics, Marshall decided that the best strategy was to hold his tongue. He did not attack Davis for putting a happy face on the horror of racial discrimination. Instead, Marshall spoke about the well-being of black students. He said that segregated schools, in addition to being inferior facilities, acted to destroy the self-respect of black children and to devastate their emotional well-being. Building on the argument, Marshall said that segregation undermined the self-confidence of black children and their standing as equal citizens of the Republic. Segregated schools were the basis for "humiliation" for Americans with black skin, the NAACP lawyer said, and it was not a matter of "theoretical injury" but "actual injury." Later he came close to the edge of anger when he said that anyone defending separate schools was showing "an inherent determination that the people who were formerly in slavery . . . shall be kept as near that stage as possible . . . This Court should make it clear that this is not what our Constitution stands for."

This was the heart of the argument in the *Brown* case. And the Supreme Court, under Chief Justice Earl Warren, ruled 9–0 in favor of Marshall's argument. On May 17, 1954, the Court decided that "to separate [black children] from others of similar age and qualifications solely because of their race generates a feeling of inferiority as to their status in the community that may affect their hearts and minds in a way unlikely ever to be undone." Chief Justice Earl Warren, who read the decision from the bench, concluded that "in the field of public education the doctrine of 'separate but equal' has no place."

The decision handed down by the Warren Court was especially shocking to President Eisenhower. Warren's appointment upon the death of Chief Justice Vinson was Warren's reward for his work in California helping to secure Eisenhower's nomination for the presidency in 1952. Based on Warren's actions prior to and during World War II, Eisenhower was confident that he was appointing a rather conservative chief justice. No one could have predicted that the lawyer who argued the 1944 *Korematsu v. United States* case, which upheld President Roosevelt's order of internment for Japanese Americans, would, almost ten years later as the newly appointed chief justice of the Supreme Court, launch the campaign in support of overturning *Plessy*. As California's attorney general, Warren had, in the wake of the Pearl Harbor attack, demanded the evacuation of Japanese Americans from the West Coast and directed the preparation of maps depicting all Japanese-owned lands in California. It was Warren who called on the state's district attorneys to enforce the Alien Land Law against Japanese landowners and argued that the presence of Japanese in California provided the opportunity for a repetition of Pearl Harbor. The future chief justice had been a staunch advocate for the exclusion of all Japanese from within two hundred miles of the California coast.

The *Brown* decision was especially shocking given that it appeared to be thoroughly inconsistent with Warren's actions in California. Prior to Warren's ascension, the Court was deeply divided between those justices who advocated a more active role for the Court and those who supported judicial restraint. Warren immediately recognized the importance of the case and insisted that it be decided unanimously, launching a charm offensive to win over the one or two most difficult members of the Court. He proved to be very skillful at "massing the Court" and securing consensus, most evidenced by the unanimous decision in *Brown,* his first case as the newly appointed chief justice.

The *Brown* case is the landmark Supreme Court decision of the twentieth century that marked the first in a long list of judgments displaying a more active Court in the defense of individual rights as no other Court before it.

3

THE LEGAL LANDSCAPE

Brown, **Yea or Nay?**

If asked whether the *Brown* decision had a positive or negative impact on the United States the vast majority of African Americans, and most people of good will, would say yes. After all, how can it be a bad thing for the Supreme Court to eviscerate the pernicious "separate but equal" doctrine?

Yet there are continuous crosscurrents of *Brown* criticism even among opponents of enforced segregation. Yes, the Court's imprimatur had to be removed from the doctrine of white racial supremacy. However, almost all of us have heard of, or experienced, the support and special attention devoted to black students by black teachers and administrators in small black schools or historically black colleges. Additionally, there has been an undercurrent of intellectual criticism of the reasoning (as opposed to the result in *Brown*) as well as a bolder assertion that the federal courts and other branches of government have never been fully committed to following through on the promise of educational equality offered in *Brown*. Professor Ogletree brings these crosscurrents to the surface and finds more merit than some might expect.

—TAVIS SMILEY

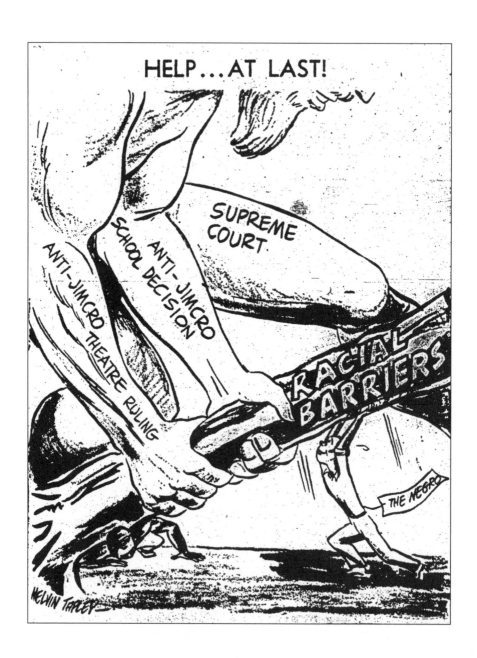

All Too Deliberate

CHARLES OGLETREE

The remarkable feature of *Brown v. Board of Education*[1] is the manner in which the first decision, *Brown I,* has come to define modern American democratic liberalism, while the second decision, *Brown II,* has come to dominate the response to education reform. The *Brown I* decision made possible the institutional equality first promised in 1776 with the Declaration of Independence ("All men are created equal")[2] and again in 1865 with the ratification of the Thirteenth and Fourteenth Amendments to the U.S. Constitution.[3] Yet *Brown II* defined the manner in which the United States was to respond to that rededication of our country to the equality ideal. *Brown I* ensured that integration was made a legal imperative, while *Brown II,* with its hesitant decision to proceed "with all deliberate speed,"[4] ensured that the legal imperative did not translate into a social imperative. Almost immediately, "massive resistance" followed as a legal and social imperative, lasting from Governor Faubus's appearance on the steps of Arkansas University[5] to the Boston busing crisis of 1975.[6]

Perhaps the most dispiriting aspect of the legacy of *Brown II* is the virtual resegregation of our education system. The pivotal 1995 decision in *Missouri v. Jenkins*[7] enabled new school districts created by white flight from urban areas to hoard funding for school districts rather than share them across a state or county. In turn, urban school districts became chronically underfunded, crippling the education of poor urbanites in general and minority students in particular. The result has been the resegregation of school systems, aided and abetted by the Supreme Court's federalism doctrine, which has ended court-ordered attempts to preserve integrated school districts.[8] As a result, even aggressive affirmative action is barely keeping minorities in elite institutions.

The speed with which we embraced the society *Brown I* made possible has indeed been all too deliberate. It has been slow, cautious, wary.

Each step has been taken painfully and at great cost. Yet the speed with which we have embraced integration has *not* been deliberate, in the sense of thoughtful or reflective. Response has been emotional and instinctive, on both sides of the debate. These reactions, anticipated and epitomized in *Brown II,* are the real legacy of *Brown I.*

Brown and Enforced Racial Amnesia

The decision in *Brown I,* ending segregation in our public schools—and by implication de jure segregation everywhere—is justly celebrated as one of the great events in our legal and political history. Precedent did not compel the result, nor was the composition of the Court indicative of a favorable outcome. After a vote was taken in 1953, when the case was originally held, the outcome was (according to some sources) 5 to 4 against the plaintiffs, with Chief Justice Vinson holding the deciding vote. Later that year, however, in a turn of events in which Justice Felix Frankfurter claimed he could see the hand of God, Vinson was dead and a new chief justice, Earl Warren, had been appointed.

President Eisenhower's appointment of Warren, one of his major political allies who had been attorney general, then governor of California, did not suggest a change for the Court. Warren was the attorney general who had argued for the result in *Korematsu v. United States*[9] in 1944, the case that ratified the internment of Japanese Americans for the first years of World War II. That decision was authored by another still-sitting justice, an Alabamian, Hugo Black. What most observers, Eisenhower included, did not know was that *Korematsu* had scarred Warren, a Californian who was already on the liberal wing of the Republican ticket. Warren recognized the importance of *Brown* because of the consequences of *Korematsu.* He not only sided with the plantiffs, he further insisted that it be decided unanimously to send a clear message. Warren launched a charm offensive to win over the most difficult members of the Court. By May 17, 1954, Warren had his unanimity but at the cost of a strong statement condemning the practice of segregation.

As an expression of moral rectitude, *Brown I* was the least the Court could have done, and in its subsequent decision it did even less. To obtain the requisite unanimity, the Court in *Brown I* bent over backward to accommodate southern white squeamishness on the morality of segregation. To avoid offending the white segregationists, the Court eschewed identifying segregation as immoral or evil. Instead, Warren demanded that the opinion be "nonrhetorical, unemotional, and, above all, nonaccusatory."[10] To identify segregation with evil, Warren and the rest of the Court feared, would be to provoke a massive rift between South and North and risk the legitimacy of the Court.

Forgotten—or, at least, discounted—were the plaintiffs and the class of citizens their claims affected. *Brown I* barely addressed the almost 100 years of Jim Crow suffering piled upon the 250 years of slavery that African Americans had already endured. As a sop, gesturing toward the effects of that suffering, Warren included a footnote on the psychological damage inflicted by segregation.[11] Exhibiting what Professor Randall Kennedy has identified as "racially selective patterns of emotional response,"[12] it is fair to say that the Supreme Court "showed an egregious disregard for the sensibilities of black Americans" and "has been careful to avoid hurting the feelings of whites."[13] And if the Court's attitude is one of solicitude toward whites in *Brown I,* by *Brown II* one can justifiably say "there is no hint of solicitude for the feelings of Afro-Americans. The Court made no attempt to assuage the inevitable anger and anxiety that the decision would generate within the black community. The rhetoric of the opinion displays . . . complacency [toward the feelings of African Americans]."[14]

In overaccounting for the feelings of southern (and many northern) whites and in refusing to describe segregation as an evil, the decision ignores the restorative function and capability of the legal system. Individuals do not come to the courts simply to obtain monetary or injunctive relief; they also come to see a decision rendered that vindicates the justice of their struggle and properly accounts for and condemns the injustices they have had to endure. Certainly, as Chief Justice Warren recognized, *Brown I* offered the opportunity for the United States to start anew without dividing the nation on the question of race. But forgiveness need not include forgetfulness, and in accounting for *Brown I*'s importance we should not ignore that it enacted a collective amnesia that haunts the nation to this day.

Compare the racial reconciliation enacted through *Brown I* and *II* with that enacted by President Lincoln, faced with similar stakes, during his second inaugural address. Unlike Chief Justice Warren, President Lincoln saw slavery as a *national* sin for which the whole country was to be held responsible (and had been held responsible by God).[15] The responsibility for atonement was therefore one to be borne by the whole nation, even though the cost would be to account for "all the wealth piled by the bondsman's two hundred and fifty years of unrequited toil."[16]

The hand-wringing manifested by Warren in *Brown I* was translated into the remedy proposed by *Brown II*. African Americans were to get the rights to which they were entitled, but uniquely in constitutional law to that point, they were to get the remedy slowly, deliberately, and at the pace directed by whites. Most obviously, black communities and black jobs were to be sacrificed and surrendered when necessary to ensure the least disruption to white communities. When schools were integrated, whites did not attend black schools staffed by black teachers and with a black principal. Instead, blacks went to the better-funded white schools, ending one vital aspect of the "equalization" strategy pursued by the NAACP in the cases leading up to *Brown I*.

The Failure to Provide Equal Education

"Equalization," the strategy developed by Charles Hamilton Houston and the NAACP Legal Defense Fund, had resulted in a number of successes throughout the South. At the level of tertiary education, the strategy had enabled some remarkable victories that paved the way to *Brown*. In 1938, in *Missouri ex rel. Gaines v. Canada*,[17] the Supreme Court ruled that Missouri had an obligation to provide Gaines with a graduate education equal to that of Whites and ordered the admission of Gaines to the in-state law school. The Court later ruled that any attempts to get around the equal-protection clause by establishing a separate law school for African American students failed as a matter of law. In *Sweatt v. Painter*,[18] the Court assumed that there was equality between the two segregated facilities but that there was more involved in a legal education than a physical site. Texas could not replicate in the African American school the learning environment, the established reputation, and the alumni/alumnae contacts of the white school. In *McLaurin v. Oklahoma*[19] the Court found that the University of Oklahoma's arrangement for separate treatment within its graduate school stigmatized African American students and handicapped their ability to pursue an education.

Before these cases wound their way up to the Supreme Court, however, the NAACP achieved a number of important victories in public education funding that helped lay the foundation for *Brown*. The NAACP brought teacher salary equalization cases in Maryland, Virginia, Alabama, Tennessee, Kentucky, Arkansas, South Carolina, Florida, and Louisiana and won several important cases. These successful suits manifested in significant gains in salary equalization in the South: black teachers went from earning 50 percent of what white teachers earned in 1930 to 65 percent in 1945. *Brown* changed all that. It marked the shift from a strategy of equalization to integration that ended the distinct and unique achievements of African Americans in public education and devastated sections of the African American middle class.

Avoiding Integration

If *Brown I* signaled the end of equalization as a permissible educational strategy, then *Brown II* indicated that so far as the legislature was concerned, integration was to be pursued with hesitation. The executive quickly followed suit. President Eisenhower accepted the *Brown* decision but stated, "The Supreme Court has spoken, and I am sworn to uphold the constitutional processes in this country, and I am trying. I will obey." He emphasized that integration should happen slowly, and it did.

As early as July 1955, the mettle of *Brown* was tested in the courts in the remanded case of *Briggs v. Elliott*.[20] In South Carolina, Judge James

Parker, speaking for a three-judge federal district court, issued a ruling that threatened the force of *Brown*. The panel stated that the Supreme Court did not mean that "states must mix persons of different races in the public schools. . . . What it has decided and all it has decided is that a state may not deny any person on account of race the right to attend any school that it maintains. . . . The Constitution, in other words, does not require integration. . . . It merely forbids the use of governmental power to enforce segregation."[21] The panel also gave a clue as to how states could maintain segregation: "[I]f the schools which it maintains are open to children of all races, no violation of the Constitution is involved even though the children of different races voluntarily attend different schools, as they attend different churches. Nothing in the Constitution or in the decision of the Supreme Court takes away from the people freedom to choose the schools they attend."[22]

Within two years of the *Brown I* decision, Senator Harry Flood Byrd of Virginia coined the phrase "massive resistance." Ninety percent of the congressional delegation from the South signed a "Southern Manifesto" renouncing *Brown* as a "clear abuse of judicial power" and vowing to reverse it by using "every legal means" at their disposal.[23] From the White House to the city councils of the smallest towns, those in power found ways to either subtly defer or defiantly oppose desegregation. Alabama, Virginia, and Georgia tried to deactivate the *Brown II* order by passing laws that forbade local authorities to desegregate whether or not they were in compliance with a federal injunction.[24]

Southern cities soon learned that they had a powerful arsenal in preventing desegregation. The most powerful of these weapons was actually closing schools when faced with a court order mandating desegregation. In Virginia, the power to close the schools was at the heart of its "massive resistance" statutes. By statute, the governor was required to close any integrated public school. This power was complemented by the unofficial act of giving public money to private white segregated schools. Schools in Norfolk, Arlington, and Charlottesville were closed by the state for most of the 1958–1959 school year. In Prince Edward County, public schools stayed closed for several years while a white private academy prospered with state-supported grants.[25]

VOICES OF THE ERA

John Stokes was one of the student leaders who on April 23, 1951, walked out of Robert R. Moton High School in Prince Edward Country, Virginia, protesting the separate but very unequal conditions of their school. Led by sixteen-year-old Barbara Johns, niece of civil rights pioneer Reverend Vernon Johns, the student strike lasted for two weeks. On May 23, the parents of the high school students and the NAACP filed suit to desegregate the public schools in Prince Edward County. Known as *Davis v. The County School Board of Prince Edward County*, this was one of the five school desegregation cases that comprised the Supreme Court hearing on *Brown v. Board of Education*.

> *Barbara Johns served as our spokesperson and our leader; she came to us with a cause. We developed it, and it worked. There were some persons in the community who were against what we were doing, so we developed our own nucleus and caucus groups. We started in October and did not pull this thing off until the day of the primary in 1951 at ten o'clock in the morning.*
>
> *The conditions were deplorable at Robert R. Moton High School. The school we were attending had been built to hold 180 students. On the day we walked out, the population was 455. They built tarpaper shacks to accommodate the overflow. Most tarpaper shacks were worse than barns because they were poorly insulated. It rained in there, and in many cases persons who were sitting next to the stove in the wintertime burned and the persons who were sitting in the farther corners froze. We knew, in terms of the power structure, that everything was programmed for us to fail. As we looked at the twelve or thirteen wooden buildings in the*

John Stokes

county for blacks and then at the brick buildings for whites, there was no comparison. The black students had outdoor toilets, and most of the time those small schools were built on properties that were adjacent to churches where there was a well outside. If you compare in 1951 a school's assessed value, $330,000 may have been the value for the black school and $1.2 million for the white school. That is about an $870,000 difference. They told us it was equal; it was not.

There were 117 students whose names appeared on the petition, and 6 or 7 parents signed. The parents risked everything. They stood like Seminoles in the wild behind their children so that we would have equality. That was the strength we had, going full force with the NAACP to get integration. The tension really arose in Prince Edward County, a lot of those who were involved were threatened and they lost homes. About two weeks after we had gone on strike, blacks were ready to load their guns, ready for a war. It was as simple as that.

A number of southern states passed pupil placement laws designed to block transfers between white and black schools. Six states authorized the closing of public schools under the threat of integration, four states provided financial assistance to white students who attended private schools to avoid court-ordered desegregation, and many of the Deep South states weakened their laws on compulsory attendance, teacher salaries, student transportation, and the terms of teachers'contracts.[26] Each of these laws was an attempt, at the very least, to delay desegregation by forcing courts to peel away a layer of state government that had been "interposed" between the local schools and the courts.[27] States also realized that they could manipulate attendance zones and otherwise control the racial composition of schools down to the very classrooms.[28]

The resistance to integration was not limited to the South. Northern and midwestern cities that wished to limit integration already relied heavily on their authority to draw boundary lines that reflected the racial characteristics of the neighborhoods rather than the locations of the schools. Southern school officials soon followed their ways. For example, when the city of Charlottesville, Virginia, was faced with court-ordered desegregation, it divided itself into six elementary school zones. The lines of the "black" zones were so carefully drawn that the area included almost all of the black students who had applied to go to previously all-white schools.[29]

One Generation of Integrated Education

The southern school systems remained almost completely segregated for a full decade after *Brown* was decided. By 1964, only one-fiftieth of southern black children attended integrated schools.[30] In the North, many school districts were equally harsh. Many refused to provide racial data that could be used to measure segregation, and as a result, northern segregation remained unaffected until the mid-1970s.[31] Some states, such as North Carolina, practiced token integration and positioned themselves to be somewhat conciliatory and thus escaped judicial scrutiny of their public education systems and actually experienced less integration than those states that opposed integration more adamantly.[32]

School integration was not achieved until the advent of busing, and even then only at great social cost. As late as 1975, Boston refused to consider integrating the local school system despite coming under the ambit of the U.S. Constitution and the Massachusetts Racial Imbalance Acts (both of which mandated an end to racially discriminatory schooling). The Boston busing crisis was sparked by a federal district court's adoption of an NAACP-sponsored plan for the Boston public school system that attempted to achieve a racial population in each school that roughly corresponded to the population of whites, blacks, and others in the community. To achieve this goal, the Boston litigation mandated the busing of about twenty thousand children. In fact, the court ordered the city to transform the school system from a racially discriminatory "dual" system to a unitary one, and in the process to consider a variety of methods for so doing. These methods included "busing, the pairing of schools, redistricting with both contiguous and noncontiguous boundary lines, involuntary student and faculty assignments, and all other means, some of which may be distasteful to both school officials and teachers and parents if necessary to achieve a unitary school system, they must be implemented."[33]

The white community mobilized in the thousands to oppose this plan. In South Boston, hundreds of praying mothers marched through the streets with their rosary beads in hand[34] and members of the predominantly Irish community would gather in front of their neighborhood high school singing the neighborhood anthem, "Southie Is My Hometown."[35] In Charlestown, hundreds of residents staged a "funeral procession" in the pouring rain to mourn what they said would be the city's death if court-ordered busing was not abolished in the next five years.[36] The white junior class from South Boston almost entirely boycotted busing to the African American Roxbury neighborhood. Many transferred to Roman Catholic or other private schools; others used relatives' addresses to go to high schools in other neighborhoods; and many more just dropped out.[37]

The office of the local chapter of the NAACP was firebombed.[38] White and black students got into a variety of physical altercations. At South Boston High, a black student stabbed a white student; a mob of at least fifteen hundred protesters trapped all the black students inside, chanting, "Give us the niggers, give us the niggers, send 'em back to Africa." Three white men were arrested for assaulting police officers outside of South Boston High.[39] One mob, awaiting buses carrying black students from Roxbury, had with them a dummy dressed in blue overalls bearing a sign "Nigger Beware."[40] During the worst of the crisis "more than sixteen hundred state and city police [were] on hand to maintain 'high visibility' on the streets and in the schools, and a hundred riot-trained U.S. marshals assisted. A special team of Justice Department officials [were] there to observe; even the 82nd Airborne Division of the U.S. Army [was] ready to move in from Fort Bragg, North Carolina, if the city exploded."[41]

From the Boston experience, which was replicated all over the nation, it is fair to say that the country achieved an integrated public school system only around the mid-1970s. It took twenty years from *Brown* for the nation to achieve integration. But as the Boston experience made clear, large sections of the population, North and South, never embraced integration. During the past thirty years, large numbers of Americans, perhaps even a majority, have acted to subvert the ideal of integration announced in *Brown I.*

Integration has failed de facto and may no longer be required de jure. A major cause of the end of the *Brown* ideal has been a Supreme Court that, once Warren retired, wasted little time undoing the few gains that were so painstakingly and "deliberately" achieved.

The Failure to Ensure Integrated Education

The last educational segregation case in which the Court spoke unanimously, *Swann v. Charlotte-Mecklenburg Board of Education* (1971), laid the groundwork for the major school busing initiatives of the 1970s. It proved, however, to be a double-edged sword. The Court's distinction between de jure and de facto school segregation—involving schools that were not segregated by laws, which *Brown* struck down, but were, in fact, segregated—provided the means by which to dismantle the efforts at integration.[42] There must be some purposeful intent to segregate in order to uphold a court-ordered desegregation plan that included busing.[43] When such a constitutional violation is found, busing is an appropriate remedy.[44] The seed that would grow to disembowel *Brown* is in Swann's last paragraph. This predicts that at some point de facto, or actual, segregation will no longer be caused by former de jure or legal segregation— that is, Jim Crow laws—and then federal courts will have to stand down: "At some point, these school authorities and others like them should have achieved compliance with this Court's decision in *Brown.* The system would then be 'unitary' in the sense required by *Brown.*"[45] These words would later be used by Justice William H. Rehnquist as a basis for repealing desegregation orders. In the Swann case, Chief Justice Warren E. Burger had convinced the entire Court to affirm that the instruction in

Green v. County School Board, which made affirmative "desegregation" in rural schools a requirement, only applied to de jure segregation and that "demographic patterns" could excuse de facto segregation.[46]

In 1991, as challenges to desegregation orders begin wafting up to the Court, William Rehnquist, now chief justice, seized on Chief Justice Burger's language in *Swann* to start dismantling desegregation decrees in cases where the present segregation was not a direct product of previous discriminatory intent. *Board of Education of Oklahoma City v. Dowell* was the first such case in which the Court sanctioned changes that would have segregative effects. The Court ruled that segregation could usually be the result of the board's action as long as it was not proven that the measures were undertaken with discriminatory purpose.[47] Previously the Court had explicitly applied the *Washington v. Davis* (an employment discrimination case) requirement of purposeful discrimination to challenges of school board policies.[48] Justice Marshall dissented vigorously on the grounds that effects of de facto discrimination had not dissipated, and berated the Court for "subordinating" the constitutional rights of black students to immaterial appeals to local control.[49]

THREAT TO HISTORICALLY BLACK COLLEGES AND UNIVERSITIES

There has been no more explicit example of the failure to ensure equal educational facilities than the treatment of historically black colleges and universities (HBCUs). Of the 103 HBCUs currently in existence, 15 percent are on warning or probation status with accreditation agencies. Many can barely meet their payrolls. Two—Morris Brown College in Atlanta and Mary Holmes College in West Point, Mississippi—have lost their accreditation. Grambling State University in Louisiana is on probation after auditors couldn't make sense of its accounting records.[50]

The irony could not be more pronounced. At a time when affirmative action is under attack, even from the Bush administration, those colleges that exist to support a predominantly African American student body also are under attack. It is not as if HBCUs are failing because of ineptitude. Although some are suffering from poor accounting practices, all have faced discrimination from the states in which they are located. HBCUs are funded at a lower level than other state colleges. In *United States v. Fordice*,[51] the Court found that Mississippi continued to discriminate against its HBCUs in such areas as admission standards, and such discrimination was traceable to the de jure segregation of the Jim Crow era.[52] The state's proposed solution, to close the HBCUs, was held to be unconstitutional.

In concurring with the opinion, Justice Thomas noted that:

There exists "sound educational justification" for maintaining historically black colleges as such. Despite the shameful history of state-enforced segregation, these institutions have survived and flourished. Indeed, they have expanded as opportunities for blacks to enter historically white institutions have expanded. Between 1954 and 1980, for example, enrollment at historically black colleges increased from 70,000 to 200,000 students, while degrees awarded increased from 13,000 to 32,000 . . . it [is] undisputable that these institutions have succeeded in part because of their distinctive histories and traditions; for many, historically black colleges have become "a symbol of the highest attainments of black culture."[53]

The centrality of HBCUs to black education cannot be overstated. According to Milwaukee Journal Sentinel reporter Ruby Bailey, these colleges and universities "helped educate much of the nation's black middle class. Thirty percent of blacks who hold doctorates earned them from black colleges, as did 35 percent of African American lawyers, 50 percent of black engineers, and 65 percent of Black physicians."[54] With the Bush administration supporting the demise of affirmative action at the college and graduate school level, such universities stand to become especially important at a time when many face budgetary crises unlikely to be undone by a proposed 5 percent increase in funding by the federal government.[55]

The desegregation decision in *Dowell* was the first by a newly constituted President Reagan and Vice President Bush Supreme Court.[56] The following year, in *Freeman v. Pitts*, the Court sanctioned the gradual dismantlement of desegregation decrees and empowered federal district courts to decide when unitariness—when a school district is free of all remnants of deliberate segregation—had been achieved.[57] This move by the Court to accelerate unitariness findings was critical, because under *Keyes v. Denver*, once a district becomes unitary, then subsequent segregation is not de jure—and the available remedies become severely limited.

The last significant Supreme Court desegregation case, *Missouri v. Jenkins* (1995), involved an attempt by a district court to force the state to spend more money on schools to improve educational quality and attract white students to predominately black schools as part of a remedy for past discrimination.[58] However, the Court struck down the order because the claimants could not prove that either poor educational offerings or racial segregation were caused by past de jure discrimination. Adopting a corollary to Detroit's *Milliken v. Bradley I* (which held the Detroit public school system was racially segregated and ordered the adoption of a desegregation plan for eighty-five outlying school districts because Detroit-only desegregation efforts were deemed inadequate), in 1974 the Court held that the "interdistrict goal [was] beyond the scope of the intradistrict violation."[59] Furthermore, the Court evaded the responsibility it had laid out in *Milliken v Bradley II* (1977) by permitting district courts in certain circumstances to order states to provide more resources to individual districts as a remedy for past discrimination by claiming that interdistrict remedies are justified only when aimed at individuals—not at institutions—because increasing the composition of white students does not match the harm of prior discrimination in the district.[60]

The practical effect of the Court's decisions has been the resegregation of even those school districts integrated by *Brown*. For example, before *Brown*, the city of Topeka maintained segregated elementary schools. In 1951, there were eighteen elementary schools for whites and four for minorities.[61] After *Brown*, the Topeka board adopted a neighborhood school policy that resulted in three of the elementary schools remaining all-black and two others becoming more than 20 percent black. In 1954 less than 10 percent of the elementary students in the district were black.[62]

The Kansas district court reopened the original *Brown* case in 1979, when the lead plaintiff, Linda Brown, along with other parents of school-age children, challenged the continued segregation in Topeka schools. In 1992, the Court of Appeals for the Tenth Circuit concluded—after being asked by the Supreme Court to reconsider its earlier opinion in light of recent desegregation cases—that the Topeka school system had not yet achieved unitary status and therefore was still under "incremental" supervision by the district court.[63] An earlier opinion[64] concluded that the district court had given insufficient weight to evidence of past de jure segregation and had therefore improperly found that current segregation was not the result of intentional discrimination.[65] In reaction to the 1979 suit, the city reorganized elementary school assignments to speed integration. Its first step was to close the three remaining all-black elementary schools from the pre-*Brown* era. By 1982, four elementary schools were more than 50 percent minority; two of those had been so since 1966.[66] In 1982, Highland Park North Elementary School in Topeka had the highest percentage of minority students, at 60.6 percent.[67] Highland Park North now appears to have closed.

At the 1986 district court trial, plaintiffs provided evidence of continued segregation. Although the initial district court decision dismissed the plaintiff's segregation claim, two Tenth Circuit Court of Appeals opinions and one Supreme Court decision did not. By 1993 both elementary and secondary school assignments were subject to district court monitoring. The district completed the court-ordered desegregation plan in 1999.[68] Nonetheless, the situation is little better. In 1985 only three schools in the Topeka school system were majority-minority, but by 2001 eight schools were.[69]

Conclusion

Brown I is a justifiably celebrated decision. It ended de jure public school segregation in this country—a blight that had lasted almost four hundred years and negatively affected millions of Americans, white as well as black. As a result, there is no doubt that for many African Americans, circumstances are better now than they were before the *Brown* decision. Many more African Americans, however, have been left behind. For some, the promise of integration has proved ephemeral. For others, short-term gains have been replaced by more of the same. School districts, briefly integrated, have become resegregated. Some distinctively African American institutions have been permanently destroyed, others crippled.

Standing on the verge of the transformation of affirmative action, things look as though they will get worse, not better. For all their clear vision of the need to end segregation, *Brown I* and *II* stand as decisions that see integration as a solution whites need only recognize grudgingly. Subsequent Courts do not even seem to recognize integration as any solution at all. And that, perhaps, is the worst indictment of the *Brown* decisions: their faith in progress, and their failure to see how quickly people of a different mind could not only resist, but also wait until the tide had turned to slough off the halting progress toward a fully integrated society.

4

A SIMPLE DIALOGUE

Play Is Work. Work Is Play.

If you can't take an idea and stand it on its head and play with it, then you haven't mastered it. A superb teacher, Derrick Bell takes us to another level in our conversation by posing the question, "What would have happened if *Brown* had been lost?" Suppose the Court had affirmed the viability of Plessy's "separate but equal" doctrine and declined to reach into state educational systems. Bell's experiment covers some of the same terrain as Ogletree's exploration of the critiques of *Brown,* but is the destination the same?

For those inclined to dismiss Bell's experiment as too fanciful because *Brown* was decided 9–0, remember that Earl Warren replaced the deceased Chief Justice Vinson after the Court agreed to hear *Brown* but before arguments and rulings. Professor Ogletree's contribution repeats the widely held (though unproven) belief that at the time of Vinson's death the Court was split 5–4 against the plaintiffs with Vinson in the majority. Ogletree also recounts Justice Frankfurter's comment that Vinson's death and replacement by Warren was a manifestation of the "hand of God." It grounds Bell's counterfactual supposition in reality.

—TAVIS SMILEY

The Potential Value of Losing
Brown v. Board

DERRICK BELL

A s usual, Geneva Crenshaw arrived without notice, evidently right through my home office window—as is her usual practice. I recognized her all too familiar sigh of disappointment, and there she was looking over my shoulder and reading what I was typing on the computer monitor.

"You don't have to tell me," she said by way of greeting. "Two o'clock in the morning on the day after you promised that poor editor at *Black Issues* that you would absolutely send your contribution for their book on the fiftieth anniversary of *Brown v. Board of Education.*"

I nodded. "I can tell from what you are writing," she said, "that like most civil rights veterans, you still see that decision as a victory for racial equality."

"Come on, Geneva, it did mark a watershed in our efforts, and it certainly sparked the civil rights movement that developed over the next decade."

Geneva sighed again. "Derrick, after all these years, you still don't . . ." She caught herself and smiled. "I am not here to bicker. Please stand up and give me a decent hug and then sit down and let me tell you what you should say."

I did as she requested, and in the midst of the hug I asked, "Will our relationship ever reach the point where my views matter to you?"

"They will," she responded, "when you recognize me as one of the thousands of together black women who when they care about a man, provide prophetic guidance." She gave me a light kiss on the cheek and smiled. "Now please sit down and type."

WHO IS GENEVA CRENSHAW?

I first met and began working with Geneva Crenshaw as we both represented clients with civil rights cases across the Deep South. She soon established herself as a fierce advocate, and was well known for her willingness to go South to represent blacks in rural settings where living conditions were poor and personal risk was considerable. Neither her legal talents nor her promise as a black leader and legal scholar saved Geneva the evening she was driving to a voter-registration meeting in the Mississippi Delta during what came to be known as the violent summer of 1964. She never made it. Her car, forced off the rural country road, rolled over and tumbled down an embankment. A student riding with her reported that the pickup truck that hit them while traveling at high speed paused only long enough to see that no one emerged from the demolished car. Then it sped away, the sound of gleeful laughter echoing across the hot summer night.

Those of us who knew her were shocked by the attack and outraged that no arrests were made. Geneva survived, but as a result of her injuries, she remained in a coma. Saddened by the discouraging reports on her continuing poor health, I began to speak of her in those terms of unqualified respect and affection usually reserved for the dead. Over time, the grief I felt at losing a friend had to be shared with the need to deal with life's continuing challenges. Even so, I never forgot Geneva.[1]

It is May 17, 1954. The Supreme Court is filled with officials and spectators. They expect that this morning the Court will hand down its eagerly-awaited school desegregation decision. They all stand as the members of the Court file in and take their places on the high bench. The chief justice signals that he will read the opinion that reflects the unanimous view of the nine men in black robes. Clearing his throat and taking a sip of water, he begins:

"This Court has been asked to determine whether the racial segregation of children in the public schools is a violation of the equal-protection clause of the Fourteenth Amendment. In 1896, this Court, in *Plessy v. Ferguson,* found that segregation of public railway cars was valid if the segregation policy was conducted on a 'separate but equal' basis. There is ample evidence in the records of the cases before us to conclude that the school boards have maintained the 'separate' portion of the policy, but despite measurable efforts in recent years, schools that Negro children are required to attend remain unequal, in some cases woefully so.

"The inequality of these schools would be a basis for relief in these cases were the petitioners seeking such relief. They are not. They maintain that even if the schools were equalized as to facilities, they would remain inherently unequal. A thorough search of the origins of the Fourteenth Amendment has failed to provide clear evidence of whether those who drafted and the Congress that approved this amendment intended it to encompass state-mandated segregation in the public schools.

"The petitioners, nevertheless, seek relief in the form of orders requiring the dismantling of the dual school systems in these cases and wherever similar school segregation policies are in effect throughout the South and other areas of the country. In support, they have provided extensive evidence by social scientists as to the harm segregation does to the hearts and minds of Negro children.

"For their part, the respondent school boards maintain that they are operating their schools under the long-settled precedents of this Court, and that deficiencies in Negro schools are being corrected as fast as budgets permit. They contend, moreover, that for this Court to find segregated schools unconstitutional would spark tremendous opposition throughout the South, opposition that would both reverse present efforts toward equalization and endanger the racial progress that has been made on a voluntary basis.

"This Court will not withhold relief for recognized violations of individual rights because of concern for public opposition. In recent years, we have ordered Negro students admitted to a number of all-white graduate schools. The orders petitioners seek here, however, are far-reaching and would affect thousands of school districts and literally millions of schoolchildren.

"It is not an accident that petitioners seek relief from this Court rather than to the state and federal executives and legislatures where because of political pressures and deeply held beliefs, such desegregation petitions would be rejected out of hand. This Court, though, must rely on public compliance with the law as we state it. We have no militia to enforce our orders. Our interpretations of the Constitution cannot exceed what the public can encompass, what other branches will enforce.

"Respondent school boards point to an earlier racial case acknowledging the limits of judicial authority that has an unhappy relevance to our decision. The case is *Giles v. Harris,* handed down in 1903. The great justice Oliver Wendell Holmes wrote the decision rejecting relief sought by Negro petitioners from Alabama who alleged a systematic policy of denying them the vote. Justice Holmes explained that if, as the black petitioners alleged, the great mass of the white population intends to keep the blacks from voting, it would do little good to give black voters an order that would be ignored at the local level. 'Apart from damages to the individual,' Holmes wrote, 'relief from a great political wrong, if done, as alleged by the people of a state and the state itself, must be given by them or by the legislative and political department of the government of the United States.'[2]

"Few would deny the racial progress made over the last fifty years. And yet we cannot ignore the depth of racial feelings that underlie the maintenance of African slavery that was recognized and protected by the Constitution's framers. The enactment of the Reconstruction amendments ended slavery and transformed the former slaves into citizens. Even so, the continuing racial hostility manifested itself in the form of segregation that, with this Court's approval, has persisted and flourished since the end of Reconstruction, officially in the South, unofficially but hardly less efficiently in much of the rest of the country.

"Petitioners are earnest in their appeals, but we cannot in good conscience provide them with a victory in this Court that, rejected by the nation, could worsen the plight of those they wish to help. The pledge in our flag salute promises 'liberty and justice for all.' This Court recognizes but on its own cannot bridge the serious disparities between that ideal and the lives of Negroes in this country.

"That said, it is within our authority to ensure that the separate but equal standard in *Plessy v. Ferguson* is fully enforced. We will thus return these cases to the lower courts with orders requiring that Negro schools be equalized with their white counterparts as to facilities, resources, teacher and administrative salaries, and all other aspects of the two school systems. We can do no more under the law and our understanding of the limits of our enforcement powers. And under those standards, we can do no less."

Geneva stopped dictating and I stopped typing and looked back, ready to protest. "Derrick, I know you don't like even the suggestion, but think about this. Just take a moment and consider how black people back in 1954 might have reacted to losing the *Brown* decision in ways that might have turned an apparent setback into a determination to push harder for civil rights."

When, after several minutes, I had said nothing, Geneva pulled up a chair beside mine. After all these years, she was still as black as anyone I know. Her powers of understanding American race and racism were as sharp as ever.

"Well, what would have happened in addition to initial disappointment?" I shook my head.

"I have some hints to get you started. What happened after the Supreme Court declared the death penalty unconstitutional in 1972 as a violation of the Eighth Amendment's 'cruel and unusual punishment' clause?"[3]

"That's easy, Geneva. The Court was subjected to widespread criticism from proponents of capital punishment, who organized and pushed state legislatures to enact changes in their capital punishment laws intended to meet the defects that underlay the Court's decision. The decision caused a temporary halt in executions, but four years later, the Court approved a redrafted statute that a Court majority found met its mandate.[4] Executions began again, and in spite of reasoned opposition, they have continued."

Geneva nodded, waiting for me to see the connection. I didn't. "Here is another hint, Derrick. What happened after the Supreme Court found in 1973 that pregnant women have a limited right to choose whether or not to abort or carry their pregnancy to term?"

"That case was *Roe v. Wade*,[5] and again it sparked tremendous opposition from conservatives who organized into politically potent 'right to life' groups who not only harassed women seeking to utilize health clinics, but also were able to make the abortion issue a test of support for political candidates and even Supreme Court nominees. By the 1990s, changes in the Supreme Court's membership made it likely that *Roe v. Wade* might be overruled. In a 1992 case, *Planned Parenthood v. Casey*,[6] the outcome of *Roe v. Wade* survived in a close 5-to-4 vote, but its protection was seriously reduced, and the obstacles women had to overcome to exercise their choice to have an abortion were substantially increased."

"No one will doubt that you are indeed a law professor, Derrick," she said. "Now that you have presented a quite impressive summary of what happened to two major Court decisions that were unpopular with an organized portion of the public, can you see the relevance to the *Brown v. Board* decision?"

"The obvious connection, Geneva, is that if the Court had ruled with the black petitioners in *Brown*, those opposed to the decision would have done what, in fact, they did do. What became known as 'massive resistance' swept across the South. The politicians shouting 'never!' the loudest were elected to office. Billboards urged the impeachment of Chief Justice Earl Warren. Congress was silent on the subject, and President Eisenhower, while making his opposition to the decision known, sent troops into Little Rock. This action was less to support school desegregation than to uphold federal authority."

VOICES OF THE ERA

Virginia state senator **Henry Marsh** was president of the student government association at Virginia Union University in 1954 when the Virginia General Assembly began its deliberation on massive resistance. He was the only student to address the body, speaking against massive resistance. In 1966 he launched his thirty-eight-year political career that includes successful runs for the Richmond City Council, where he became the first

African American mayor of Richmond. He also has served successive terms as state senator.

At the time of the decision I was a college student at Virginia Union. I worked as a dishwasher in a restaurant in the evenings after school five nights a week, six hours a night. Prior to the decision, the white high school students who worked at the restaurant were friendly with me. We all spoke to one another until that day when I noticed the high school students staring at me in a strange way. I wondered what was wrong until I turned on my radio to hear that the U.S. Supreme Court ruled that segregation of public education was illegal, that it was a violation of the equal protection rights of Negroes, and public schools could no longer operate under this basis. I realized then why they were staring at me; they looked at me in a different light after that. I was exhilarated. The constitutional rights of African Americans had been vindicated by the Supreme Court of the United States. I kept that feeling for quite a while. I went back to my dishwashing machine and to my studies. My life didn't change right away, but those students never looked at me in the same way after the decision came down.

I read in the newspaper that the Virginia General Assembly was going to consider a law that would permit the diversion of public funds to segregated nonsectarian schools. It wasn't right, so I decided to go down there and speak out against it. I was president of the student government at Virginia Union then, and I was the only student among the thirty-seven speakers. It was a joint section of the General Assembly and most of the speakers were African American leaders. I pointed out that it wasn't fair for the state to divert public funds to private segregated schools because the state was supposed to represent all of the people. That action would cause segregation to remain enforced, and we had waited so long for desegregation to occur. I chastised the legislature because they were supposed to be examples for the rest of us and they were not to participate in something that shows disobedience to the law. When the Supreme Court ruled that separate but equal had no place in public education, that meant that racial segregation had no place. They might not have used the word "desegregation," but the action they took proscribed the end of racial segregation. From my interpretation of the decision, it was clear that the Supreme Court was mandating that racial segregation could no longer exist in public education, and by implication, in other areas of public life as well.

Among the speakers at the General Assembly was Oliver W. Hill, who represented the NAACP legal staff. Oliver came to me after I finished speaking and told me how much he liked what I said. I told him that I wanted to be a lawyer just like him, and he offered me a job right there. I hadn't yet gone to law school but Oliver, being a good judge of character, offered a job, and I accepted. For the remainder of my college days and throughout law school I knew what I wanted to do. That chance meeting, that intuition to go down to speak, changed my life. I would probably never have ended up working with Oliver Hill, and I certainly would never have had the nerve to ask him for a job.

Brown was perhaps the most significant decision made by the Supreme Court in the twentieth century. It marked the end of the legal justification for racial inequality and the beginning of the march toward legal equality. Brown v. Board rang the death toll for the doctrine that was created in Plessy in 1896 until 1954.

Students going to school after Brown had very little appreciation for what segregation in public education really meant. It was difficult to be subjected to racial segregation, not only in public education but also in public transportation, among other aspects of public life. The idea of students being educated in a one-room school with seventy-five or eighty students across six or seven grades and only one teacher seems foreign to the average student today. This is what I experienced in grades one through five. She taught all seven grades at one time. Most young people today have a teacher for each grade or maybe even several; obviously they get much more direct input.

We had to fight for deseg-regation in all aspects of public service. It was very demeaning to see my sister give her seat to a white person when we rode the bus to school. I once went to Miami to attend an Alpha Phi Alpha convention when we stopped to go to a restroom and use the water fountain at a service station. We were

Senator Henry Marsh

advised by the service station attendants that niggers weren't allowed to use the water fountains. Niggers weren't to use the bathrooms either, so we were turned away in many places, in Georgia and other southern states.

The decision to attack public education by the tacticians of the NAACP Legal Defense Fund was critical because it was the key to assimilation into society, to progress, to jobs, to exposure. I think it was perhaps the most important area of all of them. If the NAACP had to retain segregation in public education, we would have been stifled from all of the other goals of the civil rights movement. However, the one problem encountered was the delay that the Supreme Court imposed. Instead of requiring immediate fulfillment, the Supreme Court built in a delay, which they called the order of deliberate speed. Constitutional rights are personal and immediate, so heretofore, if you had a constitutional right, the Court had to immediately vindicate it. But in the case of Brown, *the Court built in a delay that essentially meant they could take their time. This enabled the southern states to come up with alter-natives to public education. It gave them time to make adjust-ments before desegregation occurred so that they could establish alternative private schools. This almost overturned the impact of the decision, and we haven't yet achieved economic parity. There is still widespread housing discrimination. There is discrimination in the administration of justice, we have racial profiling, and more important, the economic pie hasn't been shared. In the corporate boardrooms of America, minorities are very scarce, and if minorities are in there, they usually won't rock the boat. We have a long, long way to go.*

We're still trying to convince the General Assembly in Virginia that we have an unfinished agenda. I had a very modest bill that promoted diversity in higher education and in elementary and secondary education that simply required the state's Department of Education and the secretary of education to identify those practices that have produced greater diversity and to circulate those indicators to others in the public education field. The bill was passed in the Senate, where I served, but it was unceremoniously defeated in the House without even serious consideration. Diversity is critically needed in the private sector, in government and everywhere.

Virginia played a major role in leading other southern states to resist the Brown decision. They set up special committees in the legislature to find the names of those who were supporting civil rights leaders. Samuel Tucker and I both defended whites and blacks who had to testify before the commission. The legislature tried to get the NAACP membership list and contribution list so they could harass those who joined or contributed money. We successfully prevented that from happening. They tried to disbar Mr. Tucker twice and he actually defeated their efforts in both cases. It was a lawless act on the part of the legislature, and now they express regret over that. We were able to get a bill through the Senate and the House, but the bill bogged down until Oliver Hill, at ninety-seven years old, fought to get it passed. Fighting against racial injustice was a gratuitous thing for me, but it also changed my life. This has been my labor of love for my entire career. I'm still doing it in my law practice and in my personal life. I'm in my thirty-eighth year of continuous selective service and I'm enjoying it as much now as I did at the beginning. After forty-one years of practicing law, I am blessed to still have a sound mind that allows me to continue to make a contribution in this way. I am looking forward to doing this for many more years.

"School equalization programs came to a halt and the federal courts did very little to enforce *Brown's* mandate for more than a decade," I said to Geneva. "As a civil rights lawyer, I handled a great many school cases in the early 1960s. With few exceptions, southern federal judges allowed school boards to use all manners of delaying tactics."

I could see that Geneva's patience, never her strong suit, was wearing thin. "Now, Professor, with this foundation of how opponents to the death penalty, abortion rights, and school desegregation were able to virtually overturn those decisions, please exert yourself and imagine how black people would have responded to a loss in the *Brown* case. And Derrick, please convey this in an opinion like the one I provided you."

"I am not sure those instances are relevant to your question. After all, polls indicate that a majority of Americans support the death penalty, and likely large numbers oppose a right to state-approved abortion. Beyond black people and a clear minority of whites, there was not much support in 1954 for a Court decision finding segregated public schools unconstitutional."

"Get with the program, Derrick. Remember, the United States had come out of a world war to preserve freedom against Nazi oppression as a world leader. Thousands of black soldiers who risked their lives in World War II were returning home. Many of them must have been determined not to return to the deeply subordinated racial status they had known all of their lives.

"Also, consider that blacks in several communities had not waited for *Brown* before beginning an active quest for voting rights and an end to segregated public facilities. The Montgomery bus boycott began the year before *Brown* and had been in the planning stages for a long time prior to that. Because of courageous black plaintiffs backed by the NAACP, the courts had struck down white primaries and other obstacles to black voting, all before the *Brown* decision."

"I acknowledge that black efforts in opposition to racial oppression have a long history, Geneva, but I am not sure I see how a major defeat in a decision as important as *Brown* would have helped rather than discouraged those efforts."

"I love you, Derrick, but you and so many other black leaders lack vision and imagination. You have principles, God knows, but you confuse principles with the tactical ways in which those principles might be turned into real and lasting gains."

"I am not sure I get it."

"Because to paraphrase the old hymn, you woke up on the morning of May 17, 1954, with your mind set on school integration as the means of ensuring equal educational opportunities for black children. Had the Court turned you down, I assume you and the other lawyers would not have resigned your positions. I would hope you would have recognized the opportunity in the Court's commitment to bring about equality in Negro schools. That was not the victory you sought, but it was—given what has happened over the past fifty years—perhaps a greater victory.

"You had the authority under the *Plessy v. Ferguson* precedent that the school board lawyers were defending to upgrade Negro schools while keeping in place the teachers and principals and community support that had enabled many black children to learn and go forth from unequal schools to improve their lives."

"You forget, Geneva, that the NAACP had experienced mainly frustration in their efforts to get courts to enforce the separate-but-equal standard even as to matters as basic as teacher salaries."

"True, but that was prior to the Court's adverse ruling in the *Brown* decision. The Court's recognition that it could not enforce a desegregation order would perhaps have moved it to vigorously enforce its school equalization mandate."

"'Perhaps' is a key word there."

"Derrick, you sound as though we are having this discussion the night before *Brown* was handed down, not fifty years later, with more black children in schools that are both segregated and inferior than ever before and with the life chances of so many of them hardly better than they were in the worst periods of segregation.

"Civil rights lawyers spent decades trying to integrate schools with whites who would do anything to get their children safely away from any such possibility. They assumed that the presence of blacks or more than a token number of them would undermine educational quality and increase the physical danger their children would face. They were wrong in many instances, but fear won out over everything, including the court orders of well-intended judges who tried to make racial balance and busing plans work."

"What about the morale value of the *Brown* decision?" I asked. "Here, for the first time, the Court was admitting that segregated schools were wrong and in violation of the Constitution."

"Did slaves really need Lincoln's Emancipation Proclamation to leave the plantations and follow the Union army as it marched through? Of course not! They didn't know what freedom might bring, but they knew their lives under slavery all too well. Similarly, by midcentury, black people were disgusted with segregation in all its forms. Protests motivated by that disgust moved them to risk jail, physical injury, even death to mount the protests that brought down most Jim Crow signs long before Congress enacted the Civil Rights Act of 1964.

"We should have listened to W. E. B. Du Bois' 1933 admonition that black children neither needed separate schools nor integrated schools, that what they needed was an education. If we had listened, we would have taken the equalization mandate I suggested. We would have done then what so many educators are trying to do for black children now by recognizing the special problems of a still disadvantaged people and their children."

"I have been following many of these efforts, Geneva, and I must admit that the success some have achieved is impressive. And you are right; many of these schools were started after it became clear that school desegregation via racial balance and busing plans was not working."

"Then you must also be able to imagine the positive effects if this recognition had come in the wake of losing the *Brown* decision, for that is what some black educators were doing in their segregated schools.

They worked with the resources they had and designed schooling that met their students' needs. Winning the *Brown* decision, as you would put it, resulted eventually in many black educators losing their jobs in the 1960s and 1970s when their school districts complied with school desegregation orders by closing black schools."

"In other words, what you are saying, Geneva, is that at least regarding the effective education of black children, we might have gained more by losing the *Brown* decision than by winning it."

"You say it, Derrick, but you don't sound convinced. Think about it. With the conservatives in charge of the courts and able to beguile most of the country, there may be many more defeats that, with some imagination, you can turn into advantages."

I turned back to my computer and found all that we had said, properly formatted and ready to print. I looked over to thank Geneva, but she had gone as quietly as she had arrived.

5

THE TEACHERS

In the Line of Fire

Booker T. Washington and W. E. B. Du Bois did agree on one thing: education is the key to African American progress. Behind virtually every educated African American through my generation stand two folks without whom we wouldn't have made it. The first was a parent figure, usually Mom (as in my case), a grandmother, a Dad or someone from the community or extended family who inspired and kept the student's feet to the fire.

The second figure was a teacher who saw some potential in this emerging child and opened the possibilities to the world of learning. For me, that person was my second grade teacher, Mrs. Vera Graft. Before *Brown* this pedagogical figure was invariably black. As we learn elsewhere in this volume, that ratio has not changed as much as the promise of *Brown* would have suggested. However, *Brown* was the opening battle in a new campaign in education and among the first casualties were the frontline soldiers in Negro education: the black teachers. How did they cope with this challenge? That subject is addressed in this contribution by Mary Hatwood Futrell.

—TAVIS SMILEY

Robert Russa Moton High School (above) and Farmville High School (below) in Prince Edward County, Virginia, serve as but one example of the difference between segregated schools. By the 1950s, the all-black Moton High, which was constructed in 1939, housed twice the number of students than it was designed to hold.

The Impact of the *Brown* Decision on African American Educators

MARY HATWOOD FUTRELL

"In a war there must be some casualties, and perhaps the black teachers will be the casualties in the fight for equal education of black students."[1]

The invitation was quite simple: all teachers who had taught at Lyles-Crouch and Jefferson-Houston Elementary Schools and Parker-Gray High School in Alexandria, Virginia, were invited by the Alexandria Old School Alumni Association (AOSAA) to attend a special celebration in April 2002. The three schools were the ones attended by African American students prior to desegregation, and the AOSAA consisted of students who attended those schools. On the day of the celebration, approximately thirty teachers and more than a hundred former students were present. Six of the teachers from Parker-Gray High School, including myself, were there.

During the program, the former students indicated that for some time they had been discussing how to express their appreciation to the teachers who taught them, especially during the days when the school system was segregated. Several commented on how hard their teachers had made them work and how the teachers refused to accept anything less than the students' best performance, academically or otherwise. Some talked about their successes and those of their fellow classmates. These students became lawyers, doctors, judges, members of the School Board and City Council, officers in the military, business leaders as well as proprietors of businesses, entertainers, ministers, educators, and professional athletes. All credited their success to the quality of their education despite the fact that the schools were segregated, facilities were dilapidated, and access to instructional resources was not equal to that enjoyed by white students.

It has been two years since that event, but it served as my prelude to the commemoration of the fiftieth anniversary of the *Brown* decision. As we prepare for this momentous occasion, it is only appropriate that we focus part of our attention on African American educators who paid a heavy price so that African American children could have access to more equitable educational opportunities. The decision mandated educational equity and parity for African American students; it was not about equity and parity for African American educators.

I have often wondered whether the leaders who developed and implemented the strategy to desegregate America's schools anticipated the impact on black educators—teachers, counselors, and administrators. There is little indication that the strategists foresaw the enormous negative impact that, at least for the first two decades, the implementation of the decision would have on the nation's black educators. Black educators themselves could not have anticipated the fallout.

VOICES OF THE ERA

Merrill Ross was the only black principal in Topeka, Kansas, in 1954. Mr. Ross was the principal of Washington School from 1954 to 1962, when the school was closed. A former Tuskegee airman, Ross was one of the educational leaders of the black community in the 1950s. A native of West Virginia, Mr. Ross attended Kentucky State for two years and graduated from Pittsburg College. His wife attended West Virginia State College and also was a teacher in Topeka until they married. The Rosses currently reside in Topeka, and an elementary school has been named for both these educators.

There was great concern for what was going to happen to us as we moved into an integrated curriculum and program. We wondered about whether we would be given consideration according to our level of training. At Washington School our teachers had degrees or levels of training equal to or better than teachers at white schools during that period. That time was a challenge for us because there was no encouragement or invitation for the teachers to be participants in the NAACP's endeavor. The plaintiffs couldn't have realized that the teachers would not be integrated as well. They thought that all of us would be taken in, teachers and pupils. They also hadn't realized that some of the organizations hadn't even tried to look out for us. They had just forgotten us. Maybe they thought we had already been included, but we hadn't.

The teachers weren't moved into the schools very quickly. It was a gradual thing. We felt that once the students were recognized as being very well qualified, then the white parents would ask for the black teachers to come to their schools. Many of the teachers had taught here for a long time. They were up in years and unmarried, they had their roots here. I think they were just hoping and praying that things would work out. They weren't sure that they would be able to go someplace else. They were hopeful for some changes, but they just had to keep quiet and talk among themselves about their concerns.

Prior to 1951, there were four black schools: Buchanan School, McKinley School, Monroe School, and Washington School. There was a flood at McKinley School in North Topeka after 1951, and it was closed because of speculation about the condition of the facility. It was sold to a contractor and used as a storage place. Washington School was closed in 1962. After spending sixteen years there, they didn't even put a marker to show where it once existed. This was one of the schools that served black children, and they didn't even have that decency.

The teachers here were very dedicated, and they prepared those children for things outside. They knew what was coming. Many of the students who are still living say that they felt good after they were integrated because they didn't feel like they were inferior in any way because of the preparation they received from our teachers. There were a lot of black social clubs where the parents and teachers often came into contact. The sororities and fraternities were all active here. They had forums at the churches

Mr. and Mrs. Merrill Ross

in the afternoons, they had resource people in the community who would come to speak to the groups of youngsters and the elderly about health issues to finding jobs. The Washington School teachers made it a point to be as involved with their students as they could. Their students could match up with students from any of the other schools in the city. The teachers made a concerted effort to see to it that no youngster would be left behind. They were continuously encouraged to work hard for what they wanted. We just expected them to do their best.

So many of the people thought that because our children were segregated in the elementary schools that our materials were inferior, that the books were old, or that we didn't have the same books. This was advertised, but it wasn't true. There was a book selection committee with several teachers who were at integrated schools and they brought in materials that were being used in other places. I don't know where they got the idea that our students didn't have the same textbooks, because they did. Some schools may have been older and maybe their books had a little more wear and tear, but there were schools in certain areas where the parents had good jobs and helped to provide what the schools didn't have. The PTA would bring in the materials.

There were good things that came from desegregation as well as bad things. The outcome depended in large part on the faculties where the youngsters would be integrating. If the receiving school had a policy whereby all children, according to their skills, talents, and educational outlook would be given just consideration and given an opportunity to be participants, then they were easily integrated into the school program without any malice or with any type of prejudices. The fact that the students' reception depended on the training of the white teachers was always disturbing to us at Washington School. Some white teachers were very subtle and made it appear as though color didn't make any difference. Whereas with others, it was rather difficult for them to give a newcomer of a different color the same privileges and the same rights as the other children. Some teachers could be just as open and helpful, while others never could bring themselves around to it.

When Merrill first went to West Avondale, the white school, two teachers were ready to transfer. They had never worked under a black man, and they were not planning on staying there for him to give them instructions. But the board told them that if they couldn't work under him then maybe they had better find work elsewhere. Before the year was up, they were two of Merrill's most staunch supporters because they found out what kind of person he was and what he believed in, what he wanted to do for all the children. Similarly, when the teachers realized that black parents also wanted the best for their children, their attitudes also started to change. On the one hand, because of Brown we have a black superintendent, we have black people at the Board of Education who attend to curriculum issues, and we have quite a few of us who are principals. On the other hand, after integration we moved away from the community, schools, homes, and churches that served as the foundation. They prepared our children for the future. It is still an effort to acquire teachers, qualified teachers, who are free of prejudices. It is part of the American dilemma.

There are those individuals who are still subtle in a manner with those prejudices. It wasn't unusual as a child to see a cross burning on the mountain. I also saw men on horseback with the white sheets at about five or six years of age. Today we find ourselves in situations where this kind of racism isn't as obvious. The year before I retired I went to a principals' picnic. I was a little late in getting there, but when I went out on the back porch the white principals were playing Richard Pryor's That Nigger's Crazy. *I didn't say a thing at that time, I tried not to, but I was probably flustered somewhat by the fact that one of them had chosen to play this knowing that I or the other black principals would be there. When September came, I put my name on the agenda for the first principals' meeting. All summer I practiced what I was going to say to them. I remember telling them that at that picnic I was really chagrined and somewhat hurt to think that a group of professional men would resort to what I encountered that day. In my wildest dreams, I had never expected that. I'm sure this wasn't representative of the feeling toward me, but it certainly did not build good relations. I was visibly hurt but I lived through it, and I'm sure that there probably were other occasions like that. It is impossible to screen a person for these subtle forms. There are still many of them that are very subtle and devious in the things they do. Some of our students are able to rise above it and are not affected by it, but it is there in front of them. It's amazing, but for the most part it's not as bad as it used to be for our young people right now.*

Within the African American community there was euphoria when the U.S. Supreme Court ruled in favor of desegregating the public education system. However, within many white communities there was first anger and disbelief, then the delayed reaction of denial, followed by the fallout of actually desegregating the schools, characterized by massive resistance. As a result, although the *Brown I* and *II* decisions were handed down in 1954 and 1955, respectively, many school districts throughout the nation did not desegregate until almost a decade later.

One year after the Supreme Court decision, the Alexandria City, Virginia, public school district implemented a freedom-of-choice plan to assign black students who applied to attend white schools. More than three years later, on February 10, 1959, nine black students were enrolled in three traditionally all-white schools. The thousands of remaining black students continued to attend segregated schools. It was not until 1965, after the 1964 Civil Rights Act was implemented, that Alexandria actually moved to desegregate its schools. At the high school level, most black students were assigned to George Washington. A lesser number were sent to T. C. Williams, and almost none were to attend Hammond. Parker-Gray, the former black high school, became an integrated middle school but was later torn down.[2] By 1968 all of Alexandria's public schools had at least token desegregation.

Of the teachers at Parker-Gray High School, only the vocational teachers were initially transferred to T. C. Williams and George Washington. I was one of the teachers transferred to George Washington. This proved to be a strategy used by other school districts as well—to transfer the teachers only in such areas as library, physical education, vocational education, and coaching to the newly merged schools. The principals of the high schools met and decided which teachers would be transferred and which would remain in their "home" school. There was little input from teachers. To my knowledge, none of the Parker-Gray teachers lost their jobs, and no one quit (at least not in the first year). We felt that we needed to be in the schools to help students, especially African Americans, succeed.

The Parker-Gray High School coaches were assigned to George Washington and T. C. Williams High Schools. None was appointed to be a head coach. Mr. Arnold Thurmond, one of the Parker-Gray coaches, recalled that the varsity football coach was appointed assistant coach to the George Washington freshman football team, despite the fact that he had coached several championship teams during his tenure as a coach at Parker-Gray. None of the department chairs from Parker-Gray were appointed department chairs in their new schools.

Prior to the *Brown* decision, the twenty-one southern states maintained records of the number of African American teachers and administrators they employed; it was relatively easy to access these data. Other states, however, did not document this information. After the ruling mandating desegregation, all states stopped keeping records identifying the racial composition of the teachers in their districts, and many did not document the number of teachers demoted or dismissed. Other sources, however, provide some indication of what happened. For instance, much of the historical information documenting the impact of the decision on African American educators is found in the recorded histories of the American Teachers Association (ATA) and its state affiliates. The National Education Association (NEA), which processed hundreds of grievances for black educators and defended them through court cases, also was able to document some of the impact of the decision on the teaching profession. Citations from court cases filed on behalf of black educators (individual as well as class action lawsuits) also provided useful information, in addition to articles that appeared in such national magazines as *Life* and in local newspapers. Finally, interviews were conducted with educators who were teaching at the time the decision was handed down.

As I read these and other accounts and talked with teachers and administrators, it became clear that surreptitious strategies were used by school districts to purge the profession in ways that made it difficult for lawyers, researchers, educators, union leaders, or anyone else to know, much less understand, the full ramifications of desegregating schools, or its impact on educators. For example, according to histories of state teachers' organizations, states and districts used such strategies as:[3]

- Assigning only a handful of black students and one or two black teachers to all-white schools and then declaring the system desegregated. Sometimes "freedom of choice" plans were used to control the extent of desegregation.

- Firing African American teachers for exercising their political rights, such as registering to vote, or for joining the NAACP or a teachers' union, primarily the ATA and later the NEA.

- Administering reprisals to black and white teachers, even dismissal, if they spoke out in favor of complying with the desegregation orders.[4] Some districts required teachers to sign loyalty oaths to the school districts stating their support for segregated schools.

- Transferring thousands of African American teachers to all-white schools and firing thousands more "before districts actually desegregated." For instance, one superintendent in Kansas, in anticipation of an affirmative decision in the *Brown* case, sent a letter to all of the black educators in the district telling them they were not being renewed because there would no longer be a need for their services.[5] None were reappointed the next school year.

- Abolishing tenure laws where there were high percentages of black educators, thus giving administrators the right to summarily dismiss teachers with or without cause. In many of the schools that merged after *Brown,* "white teachers and principals were retained while black teachers and principals were demoted and/or dismissed."[6]

- Dismissing Black educators, even though the tenure laws were not changed. Black teachers were assigned to teach out of their content field and then evaluated as incompetent, placed in government contract positions that were contingent on funding, and denied promotional opportunities. Most of these dismissals were made under the guise of "incompetence" even when the black educators were more highly certified and had more seniority than their white colleagues.

- Implementing policies that defined the parameters for desegregating the faculties within each school. For instance, in Milwaukee, the "21-11" rule was implemented. That meant that no school could have more than 21 percent, or less than 11 percent, black teachers. The policy, which was developed by the district and the teachers' union, was intended to ensure desegregation but to disallow resegregation of a school's teaching force. A similar policy existed in such states as Alabama.

- Failing to replace black teachers who retired with other black teachers, especially in the southern states.

The transition from segregated to desegregated schools was often very difficult and filled with racially tense overtones. While there were examples of white teachers and administrators who went out of their way to welcome African American educators and befriend them as colleagues, black educators who remained in the education system most often found themselves in hostile environments where some white teachers refused to speak, much less work, with them. Others questioned the validity of black educators' teaching credentials. It was not unusual for white parents to refuse to allow their child to be assigned to classes taught by black teachers or to be disciplined by them.

In most instances, little information or professional development training was provided by the school districts to help acculturate teachers or students—both black and white—into the newly desegregated schools. Professional development focusing on teaching and learning in a multicultural environment generally did not occur until several years after desegregation policies and programs were implemented, often after racial confrontations had erupted.

An Unexpected Outcome

During the same period, another transformation took place: integration of the teachers' unions (or "associations," as they were called in the South). Until the early 1960s, most African American educators, especially those in the southern states, belonged to the ATA and its state affiliates (representing approximately 75,000 educators), while the white teachers belonged primarily to the NEA (which represented approximately 800,000 educators). The ATA was negatively affected by desegregation; its membership declined as more and more black educators were purged from teaching positions and as those assigned to desegregated schools increasingly held dual memberships with the NEA. This resulted in a merger between the NEA and the ATA in 1966. Although desegregation of schools was not intended to cause a merger of the black and white teachers' organizations, it did have that result. Today the NEA, representing more than 2.7 million educators and allied educational support personnel, is among the most culturally diverse organizations in the United States, if not the world.

Defending the Rights of Black Educators

As a result of appeals from educators in thirty-six states with high percentages of African Americans, primarily the twenty-one southern states, the NEA assumed the leadership role in defending black teachers during the desegregation era. According to a 1979 article by Samuel B. Ethridge, by 1972, eighteen years after *Brown*, more than 41,600 black educators (teachers, counselors, and principals) in the southern states had been displaced or lost their jobs. More than 50 percent of black administrators were demoted or dismissed. There were no data on how many black educators were demoted or lost their jobs in the remaining states during this same period.

The ATA and the NEA and their affiliates (before and after the merger) defended thousands of dismissed black educators whose rights were violated as districts moved to desegregate schools. Some of the cases lasted for more than a decade. The NEA raised funds through contributions from members to "protect and promote professional, civil, and human rights of educators by providing legal and other necessary assistance" to educators who were dismissed. Unfortunately and sadly, we may never know exactly how many educators suffered such consequences because many teachers were too intimidated by school officials to lodge complaints and feared that reprisals would be made against them and their families.

The story of Alice Lee Causey is a vivid example of reprisals against teachers who spoke out for justice in education. In 1956 Mrs. Causey, a teacher in Choctaw County, Alabama, was quoted in a *Life* magazine article as part of its series about desegregation, "Frustration of a Negro Teacher." Mrs. Causey told the *Life* reporter, "Integration is the only way through which Negroes will receive justice on our jobs and equal pay, then we'll be able to afford better homes and a good education."[7] A few days after the story appeared, Mrs. Causey received a letter from the superintendent stating that unless she "could provide proof to him and the members of the Board of Education that she did *not* make the statement attributed to her in the September 24 issue of *Life,* she would be suspended effective October 1.ʺ[8] Word of what she had said spread quickly through the community. Between the time the article appeared and Mrs. Causey received the letter from the superintendent, her husband's car was confiscated; soon no merchant in town would sell the Causeys any merchandise, including food. Mrs. Causey and her family left town, but returned a week later to appeal the decision. Her appeal was denied because she refused to recant the quote or to sue *Life* magazine. With the help of the magazine, some other teachers, and friends, the Causeys relocated to another state because they could no longer live in Choctaw County, Alabama. Mrs. Causey is but one example of many more black educators forced to leave their communities if they hoped to survive, much less teach again.

Considerable efforts were spent defending teachers' rights and at the same time trying to improve their status. Teachers' organizations not only defended due process rights but also endeavored to equalize teachers' salaries, stipends, and other benefits; ensure due process in matters related to hiring, transferring, promoting, or terminating school employees; provide professional development; and enhance conditions within schools.

During this same period, the federal government began to investigate the devastating impact of desegregation policies on African American educators. Under the leadership of President Lyndon B. Johnson, Congress created the Interagency Task Force to investigate the treatment of black educators under Title IV of the Civil Rights Act of 1964.[9] The federal government also began to require states to keep records of the composition of their student and educator personnel populations by race. At the same time, the NEA created a task force to gather and analyze data on this issue. Ethridge was selected by the NEA to head its task force and to be its liaison to the federal government's task force investigating the plight of black educators.

Displacement of Black Educators Hurt Black Students

Purging black educators from the teaching force basically meant that black students were placed in environments that were often hostile educationally and culturally. The absence of black educators meant that black students did not have role models to demonstrate that they, too, could succeed academically and motivate them to do so. The lack of counselors meant that black students were typically not advised to pursue a traditional academic curriculum and were herded into non-academic programs. The school environment was devoid of cultural diversity reflecting them or their history. Many black students dropped out of school, while others vented their frustrations by being disruptive, often ending up being pushed out.

Five Decades Later

Viewed from the perspective of five decades, *Brown* has resulted in considerable growth and change within the nation's education system. Today, schools are more diverse than they have ever been. Of the 54 million students enrolled in public and private elementary and secondary schools, 62 percent are white, and 38 percent are African American, Hispanic, Asian, or Native American.[10] School populations are more ethnically, linguistically, and economically diverse than ever. However, today and for the foreseeable future, the issue of class, rather than race, may be a more defining factor in determining access to education and its quality. By 2010, student enrollments are expected to exceed 55 million, with 45 percent coming from language or racial minority families, or families living in poverty. Today, 25 percent live in poverty.[11] The vast majority of those children are from African American and Hispanic families who live in the nation's twenty-five largest cities, cities where the schools are almost as segregated today as they were prior to the May 17, 1954, decision. Residential segregation has succeeded in keeping most of the nation's largest school districts racially and economically segregated.

Fifty years ago, even forty years ago, African American teachers taught almost exclusively African American students. Today many students, including African American students, as well as students in general, may matriculate through elementary and secondary schools—even college—and never be taught by an African American teacher, much less see one in their schools. Today there are more students from racial and ethnic minority groups, including African Americans, in our schools, and more are graduating. Many still need help to acquire the educational foundation needed to succeed in our global society. *Who* teaches them to meet the challenges of the future is as important as *what* they are taught.

In 1972 there were approximately 220,000 teachers from minority groups in the United States, and it was projected that an additional 210,000 were needed to achieve equity within the profession.[12] Today, more than thirty years later, America has 470,680 teachers from minority groups, 15.6 percent of its 3,022,258 teachers. Seven and one-half percent, or 227,505, of all teachers are African American.[13] Only 30 percent of the minority educators are concentrated in those twenty-five large urban school districts referenced earlier.

Almost a third of all minority teachers have taught for more than twenty years, and a significant number will retire before the end of this decade, leaving the number of minorities in the profession at no more than 5 percent, unless they are replaced with minority teachers.[14] Contrast the shrinking number of minority teachers with the growing diversity of our student population, and the situation is even starker. (The decreasing number of students pursuing teaching as a career is not unique to minority groups, but is a trend across all racial groups.)

The dearth of minorities in education is not unique to teachers, but extends to school principals and higher education faculty and administrators.[15] In addition, it is predicted that a significant majority of higher education faculty also will leave the professoriate within the next decade. These are opportunities that should not be ignored. Districts and states should use this window of opportunity not only to enhance teacher quality but also to enhance diversity within the teaching profession.

The difficulty of recruiting enough teachers from minority groups to match the increasing diversity of our student populations grows with each passing year. As a priority, we must continue efforts to recruit, prepare, and retain teachers of color within the profession and within our classrooms. However, *all* teachers today and tomorrow, regardless of their race, ethnicity, or background, must be prepared and able to teach the students who comprise our classes. Now is the time to ensure that future generations of African Americans and other people of color prepare to fill teaching and leadership roles in education.

Was It Worth the Sacrifice?

The initial impact of *Brown* on African American educators was negative, especially during the first two decades of desegregation. Black educators paid a heavy price for the nation to desegregate its schools. Black educators not only survived the aftermath of the storm but also have achieved greater heights than initially dreamed possible. Notwithstanding the declining numbers of minority educators, especially African American teachers and administrators, our influence within the education system, in the profession, and in the policymaking process has increased. We are in key positions to make a difference in education, not just for black students but also for all students.

HISTORICALLY BLACK COLLEGES AND UNIVERSITIES AND THE FUTURE OF THE TEACHING PROFESSION

As in the past, most African Americans who decide to become teachers attend historically black colleges and universities (HBCUs), or colleges and universities with high percentages of minority students. Approximately 40 percent of all African American educators receive their bachelor's degrees and initial teaching certification as a result of attending an HBCU such as Virginia State University, where I earned my degree. If the nation is committed to increasing diversity within the teaching profession, it must acknowledge that HBCUs will be critical to accomplishing this goal.

Nevertheless, more and more pressure will be placed on schools, colleges, and departments of education (SCDEs) to demonstrate that their graduates not only can meet high standards, but also are able to teach diverse student populations to meet high academic standards. We need to recognize that SCDEs have become part of the educational accountability movement and will be held accountable for the results of their graduates. Parts of that accountability process are already in place, as reflected in the federal government's requirement that all SCDEs report the pass-fail rates of their graduates, and states' requirements that at least 70 percent of graduates meet predetermined benchmarks in order to remain qualified to prepare teachers. SCDEs that fail to meet the standards will be placed on probation; lose their accreditation; and, if they continue to fail, be shut down. Closing schools of education could ultimately result in threatening the very existence of some colleges and universities.

We have been down this path before with the National Teachers Examination (NTE) and remember all too well its impact on minority teachers. All of us remember the NTE, which was perceived (correctly or not) to be another mechanism for controlling the teaching profession, and ultimately students' learning experiences, by limiting the number of minority applicants who entered the profession.

Testing students and teachers has become even more prominent and permanent in education today than it was in the 1970s, as evidenced by increasing numbers of states requiring SCDE graduates to pass PRAXIS I and II (the new NTE), and the high-stakes testing mandates for elementary and secondary school students. One obvious question is how we guarantee that graduates from SCDEs can pass the PRAXIS I and II examinations or any other assessments. But the more critical issue is how we guarantee that each teacher is able to teach all of the students in his or her class. For the first time in my more than four decades as an educator, the focus is on teaching, preparing teachers to teach more effectively, and teaching as a profession. The focus must always be on effective teaching and highly qualified, licensed teachers if we are to guarantee all students the opportunity to receive a quality education.

Schools of education, including those HBCUs, are struggling to meet these new demands. Unfortunately, state and federal politicians have not allocated the resources necessary to enable SCDEs to transform their teacher preparation programs, provide professional development for faculty, or allocate sufficient stipends or scholarships to enable schools of education, especially those at HBCUs, to compete more effectively in the recruitment of students who are highly academically prepared. This should be a goal not just for SCDEs, but it also must be a commitment of the entire university and of society as a whole.

Today African American educators are in key leadership roles at all levels of the education system and the teaching profession. The U.S. secretary of education and other key leaders within the Department of Education are African Americans. African Americans serve on federal, state, and local legislative committees as well as on state and local boards of education. We are presidents and provosts of some of America's most prestigious colleges and universities. We are deans of schools of education as well as other schools on our college and university campuses, including Research Level I institutions (those that successfully compete for external research funds and are recognized for their faculty research). Black educators also are recognized nationally as researchers and scholars. In addition, we are presidents or executive directors of such national professional organizations as the National Education Association, the Association of Supervision and Curriculum Development, the Educational Testing Service, and the National School Boards Association. In 1954 there were no black school superintendents in the United States, and we could only be principals of schools attended by black students. Today we are superintendents and principals in school districts all over the country. We are teachers certified under the National Board for Professional Teaching Standards and recognized master teachers in our nation's schools. And, yes, we are National Teachers of the Year.

Those who opposed the *Brown* decision were prepared to do all within their power to minimize its effect in achieving the goal of educational equity and parity for America's children. By removing black educators from the classroom, some of the most powerful role models of academic achievement were removed, not just for black children, but also for all children. Fortitude and perseverance have always defined us as a people—whether in the fields as slaves, in the classroom as teachers, or in the corporate boardrooms as chief executive officers. That same fortitude and perseverance must hold steadfast as we prepare for a future that will be more challenging than any other era in our history. A highly qualified and diversified teaching profession is key to educational equity, parity, and excellence for all of America's children. It is part of the fulfillment of *Brown*. That would be the greatest way to pay tribute to and honor the legacy of the thousands of black educators who gave everything so that each child in the United States could reap the benefits of equal access to high-quality educational opportunity.

6

THE LANGUAGE

Are Some More Equal Than Others?

For conversation to have meaning, the participants must have a common language. We think we understand the meaning of the phrase "separate but equal," which is the critical language of *Plessy*. We also think we understand *Brown*'s conclusion that "separate but equal" is "inherently unequal." Richard L. Wright brings a linguist's sensitivity to the nuances of *Brown*'s language, including the trenchant question of whether the Supreme Court believed that whites were also disadvantaged by being separated from blacks.

—Tavis Smiley

Exploring the Hidden Meanings in *Plessy* and *Brown*

Richard L. Wright

Language is the single most significant and powerful tool that human beings have at their disposal, and it is put to use in almost every aspect

15,248.

Supreme Court of the United States,

No. 210 , October Term, 1895.

Homer Adolph Plessy
Plaintiff in Error,

vs.

J. H. Ferguson, Judge of Section "A"
Criminal District Court for the Parish
of Orleans.

In Error to the Supreme Court of the State of
Louisiana

This cause came on to be heard on the transcript of the record from the Supreme Court of the State of Louisiana, and was argued by counsel.

On consideration whereof, It is now here ordered and adjudged by this Court that the judgment of the said Supreme Court, in this cause, be, and the same is hereby, affirmed with costs.

Per Mr. Justice Brown,
May 18, 1896.

Dissenting:
Mr. Justice Harlan

Plessy v. Ferguson

of our existence and activity in the world. Sociolinguist Teun van Dijk said, "Beyond description or superficial application, critical science in each domain asks further questions, such as those of responsibility, interests, and ideology. Instead of focusing on purely academic or theoretical problems, it starts from prevailing social problems, and thereby chooses the perspective of those who suffer most, and critically analyzes those in power, those who are responsible, and those who have the means and the opportunity to solve such problems."[1] In these words he captures several of the primary aims of critical discourse analysis (CDA).

There are connections among language, the way it is constructed, how it is used for control, and how it reflects perceptions. A basic principle in the analysis of language dynamics is its relationship to power and social inequity. Discourse often functions as a substitute for more militant or physically coercive forms of social control. Discourse analysis takes on the character of being critical if it sets about to explore and to expose language or discourse dynamics (1) from the perspective of those who have suffered most from such dynamics, and (2) by critically analyzing those in power in terms of their discourse practices. In effect, critical discourse analysis seeks to investigate and to expose social inequality, whether visible or hidden, in addition to relationships of power abuse, social control, dominance, discrimination, and other forms of selective inclusion and exclusion of others that are often used for corrective social action. Analysts must reveal how discourse functions to "naturalize" certain sentiments, understandings, and values as merely commonsense, taken-for-granted realities to make the political seem apolitical.

Any analysis of language must be sensitive to: (1) *foregrounded information,* which refers to ideas and meanings explicitly stated and emphasized; (2) *background information,* the stated but deemphasized; (3) *presupposed information,* what is never explicitly stated, but implied or suggested by what *is* stated; and (4) *suppressed information,* perspectives that are directly relevant to understanding a statement but that are neither explicitly stated nor implied in any way. These tools applied to the 1954 desegregation ruling of the U.S. Supreme Court reveal the residue of a legacy of systemic and institutional injustice.

From *Plessy* to *Brown*

The Supreme Court members of 1954 felt compelled to respond differently to racial dynamics than the Court members in *Plessy v. Ferguson* (1896), which legalized segregation of the races in all public facilities when it declared the doctrine of "separate but equal." The words "separate but equal" compelled black people in the United States to create and maintain their own communities of service and activity, including their own educational facilities.

Fifty-eight years later, these words were rejected and these "separate" facilities were declared "inherently unequal." Explicitly foregrounded are the words "separate" and "equal" in the 1896 ruling. However, it certainly doesn't take much critical reflection to observe that the word "separate" suggests a dynamic that was never the case. "Separate" suggests that we both have something: I have mine and you have yours; it presupposes that we are both *haves;* neither one of us is *have-not*. The choice of the word "separate" was highly effective in fostering the illusion that both blacks and whites had something to work with, and that neither was deficient in what the other group had available to them. It was merely separate.

The word "equal" also is interesting as it foregrounds a reality of equality that was ludicrous in the sweltering horror of 1896. The Court constructed language to legally isolate black people, to essentially abandon them to their own resources. We can presume that the belief of the justices was that blacks were so morally decadent, shiftless, and incompetent that without the active presence and involvement of whites in their faculties and institutions, their collective fate was sealed.

How wrong they were. The record clearly tells us that education in the black community during the era of enforced segregation was the period of highest academic achievement across the black community. Blacks attended all-black schools, had all-black teachers, studied with all-black classmates, lived in all-black but supportive and protective neighborhoods, understood and respected responsible authority, and mastered the educational tools needed for success in order to make valuable contributions. During segregation the black community, left to its own resources, was able to create and sustain a culture of learning that greatly benefited the majority of black students who were privileged to have attended neighborhood schools where the focus was on learning and the associated responsibility for one's own effort in the learning process.

VOICES OF THE ERA

Judine Bishop Johnson is the daughter of barbershop owner Gardner Bishop. He was instrumental in organizing the protests and legal actions that led to the desegregation lawsuit known as *Bolling v. Sharpe*. Bishop was outraged that black students such as Bolling, for whom the case is named, attended dilapidated elementary schools while white students attended the newer John Philip Sousa Junior High School. Bishop attempted to enroll eleven young black students in John Philip Sousa, but they were turned away because of their skin color. Charles Hamilton Houston, NAACP special counsel, provided legal representation for Bishop and the Consolidated Parents Group, Inc. After Houston became ill, Howard University colleague James Nabrit Jr. argued the segregation case, but the U.S. district court dismissed the case on the basis that segregated schools were constitutional in the District of Columbia. While awaiting an appeal, the Supreme Court sent word to Nabrit that it was interested in hearing the case with the other segregation cases already pending. However, the Supreme Court rendered a separate decision in this case because the Fourteenth Amendment was not applicable in the District of Columbia.

> *In 1947 I was at Brown Junior High School and we had to attend school part-time. To alleviate this, the Board of Education at that time decided to send the students from Brown to two dilapidated former white elementary schools. When my father heard this, he just became incensed. He organized parents and the Consolidated Parents Group, Inc. They closed Brown Junior High School, and for seven years my father and that group of poor*

Judine Bishop Johnson

families from Northeast D.C.—the Little People, as he called them—undertook a revolution. He was able to obtain the services—for free—of attorney Charles Hamilton Houston. Houston worked for them until he passed away.

They accomplished several things. Cardozo High School was one of the former segregated schools that they were able to integrate. Prior to that, case after case was filed for seven years, to no avail. The parents and attorneys gave speeches all over the city, and the churches became the meeting sites. Today it is easy to take for granted the school situation in Washington, D.C. However, if you look at the history, then it is easy to understand that these schools represent pinnacles of achievement for the Consolidated Parents Group along with my father, Gardner Bishop.

Segregation or separate but equal, whatever might have been the nefarious intentions of its creators, allowed black people the space for some level of self-determination. Even with secondhand textbooks and grossly underfinanced schools, black teachers produced students whose education was not merely equal to that of whites at the time, it was superior! A large number of well-prepared black people with coveted competencies were educated prior to desegregation and received their educational foundation during the era of segregation.

Honest analysis must recognize that although the words "separate but equal" or "segregation" have the ring and reminder of an objectionable and unjust condition imposed on black people, this condition also created an opportunity to create and to monitor conditions that focused on preparation and empowerment through effective education.

VOICES OF THE ERA

Andrea and Bridgette Brown are the daughters of Ethel Louise (Belton) Brown, the plaintiff for whom the *Belton v. Gebhart* case in Delaware is named. Although there were two separate desegregation cases in Delaware, the core issues were the same: black families wanted equitable school conditions for their children. Louis Redding, the state's first black attorney, represented the parents. When the children were denied admission to the local all-white schools, the parents filed *Belton v. Gebhart* and *Bulah v. Gebhart*. The cases were heard at the Delaware Court of Chancery. The chancellor ruled in favor of the plaintiffs and ordered that the children be immediately granted admission to the white school. The Board of Education appealed this decision, and the case was filed under *Gebhart v. Belton*. Although this case forced Delaware to provide access for the plaintiffs at the state level, the decision did not strike down the state's segregation law.

Our mother was seventeen in 1954 when she received the good news. She was waiting for an answer to her suit so that she could enter Claymont Delaware High School, which was three-fourths of a mile from her rural home. She was enrolled at the all-black Howard High School, where she walked a mile to catch a commercial bus, rode ten miles to town, then walked four blocks to Howard. Mom was quoted in Jet *magazine as saying, "We passed three white high schools on the way. I had a cardiac condition and that was a lot of walking and climbing hills. Even when I was in the tenth grade I still hoped to*

Andrea and Bridgette Brown

enroll. Howard didn't have business courses, so two times a week after school, I walked fifteen blocks to Carver Vocational School to take typing and shorthand. Both nights, I went home alone. Some nights it was cold and dark." She graduated from Howard the year that the Brown decision came out, but by that time it was too late to attend Claymont.

Our mother used to talk to us a lot about her heart condition. Hers was one of the first open-heart surgeries in the United States. She died in 1981. It was a blessing that she lived to be sixty-three years old. She was born with six holes in her heart. She couldn't play with us and do physical things when we were growing up; even walking was very challenging. For her to have to walk miles to school when the doctors would advise her that she shouldn't even walk up a flight of stairs is amazing. That's what makes it all so beautiful.

Education for the oppressed and excluded is always political. Blacks clearly understood that its primary agenda was empowerment for life in an unfriendly world. Given this reality, how ironic it was that the Supreme Court, consistent with the shifting mood of the nation, voted in 1954 against the legalized condition of separate but equal public educational facilities, and in so doing asserted that separate but equal was "inherently unequal." Explicit in the use of the word "unequal" is the idea that injustice is present and unacceptable. What is implicit (unexpressed) but presupposed in the same word is that the injustice is being suffered by black people, not by their Euro American counterparts. For black people not to be allowed to study in public school settings among whites presumes the latter to be better situated and more privileged. The implication is that this injustice is only to black people and not to whites. This nation has labored far too long from the absence of large numbers of African Americans and members of other disempowered groups in significant decision-making roles in American life.

The Court in 1954 was right to act against the forced social isolation it decreed in 1896, but it denigrated the educational conditions that black people created as a culture of learning geared toward intellectual empowerment against an unfriendly world, one that gave black education its social agenda, was carried forward by committed and competent black teachers, and was fully supported by black parents, black professionals, black neighborhoods, black civic organizations, and black churches. It was never education for education's sake. It was education for liberation.

What was unequal was the division of resources allocated for black education at local, state, and national levels. What was excellence was the legacy of schools under the control of the black community. This is not a call for a return to an era that needed to end an illegal institution, but a call to recognize the general decline in black control and focus on the educational agenda. As a disempowered people confronting an unfriendly world, the transition for blacks from segregation to desegregation got what the plaintiffs wanted but cost them what they had!

7

MULTICULTURAL IMPACT I

An "Invidious Comparison"

The American discussion of post-*Brown* II remedies and the contentious argument about affirmative action invariably invokes comparisons between the "poor" academic performances of African Americans and the stellar achievements of their Asian American colleagues. Are these stereotypes or scientifically supported conclusions? Where did they begin, and perhaps more important, where do they lead? Evelyn Hu-DeHart explores this "invidious comparison" with one eye on the multicultural project, and another on segregation in education.

—TAVIS SMILEY

Chinese immigrants coming to San Francisco

An Asian American Perspective on *Brown*

EVELYN HU-DEHART

Most Americans are at least dimly aware of the "separate but equal" doctrine, the reprehensible chapter in U.S. history that the *Brown* decision intended to bring to a close, and are occasionally reminded of persistent difficulties faced by African American students using education as the pathway to upward social mobility. Meanwhile, another group of minorities, Asian Americans, have been extolled for the past three decades as whiz kids and as the model minority primarily because of their impressive academic achievements in K–12 on through college and graduate and professional schools. Accompanying this seemingly benign model-minority construction is the stereotype of docile and studious Asian American students who seldom stray from their books to complain or protest.

Thus an invidious comparison has been set up between different groups of U.S. minorities that showcases a "successful" minority, Asian Americans, for the sole purpose of denigrating the character of and denying societal responsibility for the consequences of institutional racism on "failed" minorities. It is important to deconstruct this dangerous setup and recall some history that has been largely erased, namely that Asian Americans in the early twentieth century also had experienced segregated schooling. Careful analysis of the composition of the current generation of Asian American high academic achievers and suggestions for specific explanations for their success are needed without resorting to facile culturalist arguments. It is generally not known in American public opinion, not even in educational circles, that in early-twentieth-century California (where most Chinese and Japanese immigrants had settled), Asian American children, including those born in the United States and hence citizens, were forced into segregated schools. Although the practice was uneven and sporadic, and nowhere approached the extent, intensity, and persistence of segregated schooling imposed on black children in the United States, Chinese and Japanese families fought hard against what they correctly perceived as blatant discrimination. Denied citizenship by the U.S. Naturalization Law of 1790, which restricted citizenship to "white" immigrants,[1] nineteenth-century Chinese and Japanese immigrants were permanent aliens; their U.S.–born children received citizenship in 1868 by virtue of birth as stipulated in the Fourteenth Amendment.

In 1885, the San Francisco Board of Supervisors confirmed a practice, begun more than two decades prior, to keep Chinese children out of the public schools, confident they could "prove that we can justly and practically defend ourselves from this invasion of Mongolian barbarism."[2] This decision rejected the plea of Chinese parents Joseph and Mary Tape to enroll their eight-year-old U.S.–born daughter Mamie in public elementary school. The Tapes were self-described Christians and "Americanized," and Mamie was more proficient in English than in Chinese. She and her family were among seventy-five thousand Chinese then living in California, where the Chinese constituted the largest foreign-born and nonwhite community. In view of a municipal court judge's ruling that the city had no right to deny Chinese children— whose parents paid school taxes—an education in the public schools, the California legislature hurriedly opened a Chinese school, which Mamie was forced to attend. By no means uniformly copied across the state, San Francisco's model of segregated public education was adopted by several

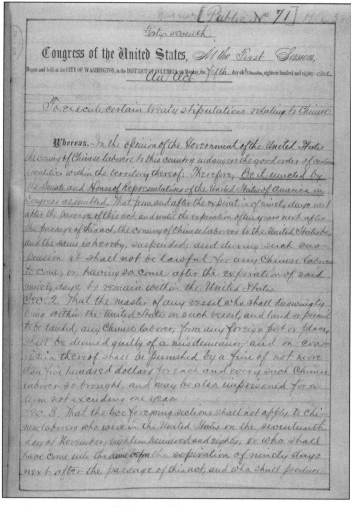

Chinese Exclusion Acts

school districts in Sacramento County. Indeed, Chinese in California were so interested in public education for their children that they actually accepted the notion of segregated schools if that was the only way their children could learn English and become Americanized. In about 1878, a group of thirteen hundred California merchants, primarily in the San Francisco and Sacramento areas—noting that they had paid more than $42,000 in various state taxes—petitioned the state Senate and

Assembly to establish "separate schools" for more than three thousand of their children, ages five to seventeen, if the state was unwilling to admit these children into schools for whites.[3]

In 1902 (six years after *Plessy v. Ferguson* legalized the "separate but equal" doctrine), attorneys for Wong Him sued the school board to allow him to attend a regular school instead of being forced to attend the Chinese school. Siding with the board, the state supreme court ruled that under the Fourteenth Amendment, the state had the right to establish separate schools for children of different races, "provided the schools so established made no discrimination in the educational facilities which they afford." In short, the court upheld the doctrine of "separate but equal."

Chinese children in San Francisco attended mandated, then de facto, segregated schools through World War II. A school study in 1947 concluded that while formal segregation for the Chinese had ended, residential segregation rendered one public school still 100 percent Chinese.[4] During this period of educational segregation, Chinese exclusion had sharply curtailed the rise of the Chinese population, thus significantly diminishing the threat of the "yellow peril."

In 1907, when ten-year-old Keikichi Aoki, with the help of the U.S. attorney's office, attempted to enroll in a San Francisco elementary school, he, too, was rebuffed by the Board of Education. The board president explained that "because of state law providing for an Oriental school, this boy cannot be admitted." He further cited Section 1662 of the California Education Law, which allowed school districts to establish separate schools for "children of Mongolian or Chinese descent." Aoki's lawyer argued that Japanese were not "Mongolians," hence could not be forced into segregated schools, but this argument was made to no avail.[5] This family's protest was in response to a board decision in October 1906 to concentrate all Chinese, Japanese, and Korean children in the "Oriental Public School" located in Chinatown. All but 2 of the city's 93 Japanese families complied, while the Korean children, a very small number, showed up. Eventually the president himself, Teddy Roosevelt, intervened to forestall a brewing international crisis, because Japan, which had just defeated Russia, a Western power, was in no mood to have its citizens pushed around. By the 1920s, apart from the few small districts in Sacramento County that maintained "Oriental schools," all but 575 of the 30,000 or so Japanese Nisei children (U.S.–born hence citizens) in California attended integrated schools.[6]

Ironically, the Nisei children were rudely yanked back into de facto segregated schools when they had to accompany their Issei parents (immigrant generation denied citizenship) into the concentration camps set up by the federal government for all West Coast Japanese during the war years. The War Relocation Authority, which operated the camps, found itself suddenly responsible for the education of some twenty-five thousand Japanese American schoolchildren. By the very nature of relocation, of course, the schools it set up were racially segregated, functioning behind barbed wire and often in unheated, flimsy classrooms, with severe shortages of textbooks, supplies, and teachers. The ever resourceful Japanese Americans soon found ways and means to improve these schools, so that when the camps closed after the war, the children returned to integrated public schools and began to thrive.[7]

In this very brief historical survey of Chinese and Japanese American experiences with U.S. public education, certain facts stand out: Asian Americans are intensely interested in education and will resort to whatever means are at their disposal to obtain education and, at the same time, fight discriminatory practices and policies, such as separate schools. At the same time, they accepted segregated schools if that was all they had.

By the late 1960s, educators began to notice these high-achieving Japanese and Chinese American students in the public schools. These students were soon joined by waves of new Asian immigrants arriving after the 1965 reforms that finally ended the long exclusion of Asian immigrants (for the Chinese since 1882, for all other Asians since 1924). Collectively, Asian American students boosted test scores, graduation rates, and matriculation at the nation's most selective public and private universities, and eventually at medical, law, and business schools as well. Within ten years of bursting on the scene, the Asian American "model minority" had saturated the media, with every major outlet from print to television vying to sing their praises.[8] The attention continues to this day and is periodically bolstered by overrepresentation on yet another list of amazing achievers. In the 2003 *USA Today*'s Academic High School All-Stars, for example, twelve of the top twenty students were Asian Americans.[9]

While many Asian American community leaders and activists, students, and educators are understandably wary of the "model minority" label, given this country's unsavory use of stereotypes against the interests of minority groups, it also would be disingenuous to dismiss irrefutable evidence of Asian American academic achievements that underlie this new social construction and to fail to examine this phenomenon.

Dramatic and profound changes to the Asian American population have occurred since the immigration law reforms of 1965. Today they are the fastest-growing nonwhite population, at a rate of more than 100 percent per decade since the 1970s. This population has exceeded 11 million, from barely one million in total when the reforms took place, to just over 4 percent of the total U.S. population in the twenty-first century. Distributed not just bicoastally but also all over the United States, this category also has become incredibly diverse, ranging from the early Chinese and Japanese to now well over a dozen ethnicities,[10] with more religions, languages, and cultural frameworks. Almost 90 percent are immigrants or children of immigrants, so transnational ties with homeland cultures and places remain strong. English is not necessarily the preferred language at home. Although most have come as voluntary immigrants after the civil rights movement, usually as families and eligible to become citizens regardless of race, some 10 percent are war refugees from Southeast Asia. The gender ratio favors women, at 51.7 percent; the median age is young, at 30.5 years; and the average family size of 3.74 is larger than the national average.[11]

These basic characteristics alone underscore the fundamental differences between today's immigrants and the predominantly male manual laborers who likely came over alone some 150 years ago. Another stark contrast is in the social environment of the two periods. Nineteenth-century Asian immigrants came into an America that was being redefined by the Civil War and the end of slavery, which then quickly morphed into a century of racial segregation that also swept in the racialized Asians. However, late-twentieth-century immigrants have benefited from the civil rights movement that dismantled American apartheid and that devised policies such as affirmative action to force open access to education, business, and occupations.

Because of immigration preferences for well-educated, highly skilled workers and professionals, many of the Asian newcomers brought with them sufficient social and cultural capital, if not a lot of financial capital, to immediately claim and invest in these opportunities. It is not unusual to arrive in the United States with a college or advanced or professional degree. Given their income, they can afford to live in middle-class and affluent suburbs, and attend school with mostly white and other Asian students, or they opt for private or parochial prep schools. Not surprisingly, these students take a large load of college prep courses, piling on advanced placement courses as fast as the College Board can create them. Since the 1970s, Asian Americans have consistently scored higher than whites and all other groups in SAT math, and were pulling alongside whites in SAT verbal by the 1990s.[12] These students also have the lowest absenteeism and the lowest dropout rates: by tenth grade, it is only 2.1 percent, compared with 4.8 for whites, 8.7 for blacks, and 10.7 for Latinos.[13] Only 6 percent of nineteen-year-old Asian American youth are not in school, compared to 26 percent of Latinos, who are at the other extreme.[14]

With this kind of high school background, no wonder Asian Americans have by far the highest college enrollment rate, at 55 percent, compared to only 36 for whites, 30 for African Americans, and 22 for Latinos. Even more dramatic are the figures for the most selective public and private universities: 39 percent of all students at Berkeley, 22 at Stanford, 19 at Harvard, 17 at Yale, and 28 at the Massachusetts Institute of Technology (MIT). It follows that Asian Americans have by far the highest percentage of bachelor's degrees, at 29 percent, compared to 20 for whites, 11 for African Americans, and 8 for Latinos.[15] Asian Americans earn 10 percent of all bachelor's degrees granted in the sciences and engineering.[16] With bachelor's degrees in hand, they move on to pursue master's, doctoral, and professional degrees in medicine (39 percent) and law (30 percent). Together with Asian foreign students, the combined group earned 21 percent of all Ph.D.'s granted in the United States in 1995. Many of the Asian nationals stay in the United States, apply for U.S. residency and eventually citizenship; their children swell the ranks of the Asian American high achievers in high school and college.[17]

These characteristics can be found primarily among the five largest groups of Asian Americans, mostly newcomers, except for the longtime Japanese Americans no longer considered an immigrant group. The others are Chinese, Filipino, Korean, and South Asian (East Indian), all post-1965 voluntary immigrants, with the children of Vietnamese refugees closing in.[18] At the other extreme are the rest of the refugee group—Cambodians, Laotians, Hmong—whose experience with schooling resembles that of many other urban minorities, black and Latino, except that these Asians' low educational attainments and general poverty are hardly ever noticed. In short, Asian Americans today exhibit a bimodal shape, but the low end has been rendered practically invisible by the broad brush of the "model minority" label that has been used to color this very diverse category.[19]

With the exception of Japanese Americans, most of whom can trace a connection to the concentration camps of World War II and to the history of segregated education before and during the camp experience, the vast majority of the Asian American high achievers are post-1965 immigrants and their children. The majority of the 2 million or so Chinese Americans are of recent vintage; hence they carry few ties to earlier generations of Chinese immigrants. Almost all the Koreans and South Asians, and most professionally trained Filipinos, are new immigrants with even fewer claims to a pre-1965 history in the United States. In these families, the immigrant ethos predominates; together with parents' high socioeconomic status (SES) measured by income and education, these two factors together and separately explain much of the students' success.

In 1997 the Educational Testing Service (ETS), which develops the SAT, AP, and other related tests under contract with the College Board, surveyed the five well-established high-achieving Asian American groups (Chinese, Japanese, Filipino, Korean, South Asian), plus the fast-rising

Vietnamese, to uncover specific factors that could explain their impressive academic achievements. The South Asian (East Indian) community is perhaps the most revealing. Almost all of them are recent immigrants, and the parents' pre-migration educational attainments and professional skills are reinforced by English proficiency, the result of an educational system derived from centuries of British colonialism. (A similar advantage can be found in well-educated Filipino immigrants, whose families became English proficient under American colonialism in the twentieth century.) Fully 87 percent of South Asian fathers have a college degree or higher, and an astounding 41 percent of them have a Ph.D.; another 32 percent have a master's degree. Of South Asian mothers, 70 percent have a bachelor's or master's, and 10 percent have a Ph.D. Not surprisingly, fully 100 percent of these parents expect their children to earn a college degree or higher, making no distinction among sons or daughters.[20]

In many ways, these Asian immigrant families confirm anthropologist John Ogbu's insightful thesis on "immigrant minorities" as distinct from "involuntary minorities." Asians are prime examples of immigrant minorities, who associate optimism with their relative recency in the United States to strive for academic achievement. Blacks and Latinos comprise the involuntary immigrant group, whose oppositional posture against mainstream (white) American culture and society, in response to persistent racism, discourages academic pursuits.[21]

Psychologists Stanley Sue and Sumi Okazaki turn this thesis around to fit the Asian American condition. They argue that precisely because Asian immigrants are cognizant of American discrimination against racialized minorities, including themselves, they respond by using educational credentials to optimize opportunities in education-dependent careers and occupations such as in science and technology, engineering, and accounting that moreover require less extensive English communication or writing abilities. In other words, Asian immigrants stress education because of its "relative functionalism" for upward mobility. It works because it helps them circumvent the effect of exclusion in non-education-dependent pursuits (e.g., sports, entertainment, politics).[22]

Sociologist Grace Kao notes that relative functionalism is the other side of the "*blocked opportunity*" theory frequently used to explain why longtime U.S. minorities, such as African Americans and Chicanos, do not place the same faith in education, given their lengthy past experiences with racism.[23] Contrary to popular assumptions embedded in the "model minority" construction, these scholars suggest that the "centrality of education for success" is not primarily an expression of Asian cultural values as much as it is a response to a perceived hostile environment.[24] In the words of Jayjia Hsia, "Cultural values certainly play a role, but economic survival remains the driving force."[25]

Many scholars wrestle with the "culture" question, but it is an elusive concept used to explain many phenomena, and it is difficult to define and test. Sue and Okazaki argue that cultural practices in and of themselves, devoid of a context in which they are deployed, carry little meaning, but when they "intersect with conditions in any particular society" at a particular time in history, these values and practices can become significant. To those who assert that cultural differences explain Asian American superior academic showing,[26] Sue and Okazaki would counter that although Asian family values and socialization emphasize the need to succeed educationally, culture gains real meaning when Asian immigrants adopt education as the major strategy to respond to a peculiarly American phenomenon of institutional and individual discrimination against those defined as "minorities" in U.S. society.[27]

Fifty years after *Brown v. Board of Education*, many of the intended beneficiaries still languish in our public education system, for reasons discussed extensively and cogently in other chapters in this volume. One minority group, however, has seemingly defied the odds by surging ahead of even white Americans in their pursuit of academic excellence. By crowning these largely new immigrant groups a "model minority," however, political pundits, commentators, and misguided educators have done them no favor. By highlighting their successes, they have helped create a backlash against Asian immigrants. Although originally included in affirmative action plans, once they were deemed overrepresented because their numbers in higher education and professional schools exceeded their percentage in the larger population, Asian Americans were quietly excluded from further consideration.

Even more insidious, however, it was discovered in the 1980s and 1990s that elite institutions such as Stanford, Brown, and UCLA had quietly imposed a top-town quota on Asian American admissions, similar to the quotas imposed on Jewish immigrant students at the front end of the twentieth century.[28] In other words, when Asian American students were able to compete as individuals against white students on the basis of the traditional meritocracy such as grades and test scores, and without the benefit of affirmative action considerations, they were subject to a higher set of standards and criteria in order to hold their numbers down in competition with white students. Viewed in this way as backlash against the relative functionalism of education as practiced by middle-class Asian immigrants, their worst fear, racism, which they thought they had so cleverly dodged, has come around to haunt them after all. Aggressive community organizing against these patently discriminatory practices—by exposing and thus embarrassing the elite institutions—has apparently curtailed, if not ended, such cynical maneuvers.

I will end on an ironic and somber note, a cautionary tale about justice, merit, and racism in school segregation. When the University of Michigan found its affirmative action practices challenged by outside forces led by neoconservatives, it veered from the compensatory justice arguments initially advanced to support the need for affirmative action toward embracing an assertion of diversity as educational necessity.[29] Some Asian American families today have a hard time accepting the diversity rationale. If a century ago Chinese parents in San Francisco protested the imposition of segregated Chinese schools, today, in the twenty-first century, the mostly immigrant Chinese American parents of high-achieving children threatened to undo racial harmony and exacerbate race relations in that city's public schools by successfully challenging Lowell High School's desegregation plan designed twenty years ago to achieve some diversity balance among the students in a multicultural city and public school system.

VOICES OF THE ERA

Duane Fleming is the son of Shirla Fleming, one of the thirteen plaintiffs in the original *Brown* case. She filed on behalf of her sons Duane and Silas,

Duane Fleming

who were not able to attend the all-white Lafayette School in Topeka, Kansas.

A lot of us had the same experiences. We've had to walk past schools that we were not allowed to go to because of the color of our skin. Education is just basic to human beings, as is a roof over your head and bread on your table. To be denied the opportunity to be educated because of the color of your skin is wrong. We'd all be much more advanced in this world if we thought of everyone as human beings.

I was a very young person at that time. I lived in an integrated neighborhood and couldn't go to school in my own neighborhood. I had white friends, Mexican American friends, American Indian friends. We were all friends, but we couldn't go to school together.

My parents and the other parents should be applauded for standing in front of the lily-white Supreme Court saying separate but equal is not good enough. They not only moved them to integrate the schools and bring white and black children together, this action also opened up the spectrum to impact principals, teachers, educators, and even janitors. People who were previously denied opportunity were suddenly able to get into places where they could earn a better living. So I give accolades to my parents, who stood up and made a difference, not only in our area but also to this whole country.

Using conventional definitions of merit—high test scores and grades—as their main argument, those parents who had failed to secure a place for their youngsters in Lowell, the city's most rigorous college prep public high school, then cried "reverse discrimination" because slots had been set aside for black and Latino students who generally did not score as high on test measures of excellence. Similar to the end of affirmative action in the University of California system when diversity in the student bodies of the most select campuses, Berkeley and UCLA, dropped precipitously while Asian American numbers rose, so, too, did Lowell become even more Chinese. Chinese enrollment was already well above 50 percent before the diversity plan was forcibly discarded. As progressive educator, Lowell parent and Chinese American activist in San Francisco Bill Ong Hing laments, Lowell could soon become practically all Chinese.[30] What Hing feared, and what the Chinese American parents could not have made more obvious with their attack on Lowell's multicultural plan, was that when diversity ended, San Francisco saw the reappearance of a segregated "Oriental" school.

8

MULTICULTURAL IMPACT II

New "Discoveries"

In the summer of 2003 the mainstream media suddenly "discovered" the growing Latino population in the United States. This epiphany was linked to the realization that, voting as a block, Latinos can affect the outcome of national political races.

The real shock of course is that the mass media, and much of the nation, have so long ignored a segment of the population with such a rich history. This history includes a hard-fought series of cases challenging educational segregation in state and federal courts. Marco Portales explores the history of Mexican American cases, particularly those that parallel the African American challenge to *Plessy*. He even ventures some views about why this story has remained untold.

—TAVIS SMILEY

A History of Latino Segregation Lawsuits

MARCO PORTALES

The U.S. Latino education story is a little sadder than the African American one, mainly because it is considerably less known. Few Americans, for instance, know about Mexican American leaders such as Alonso S. Perales, Ezequiel Salinas, Gustavo (Gus) C. Garcia, Homero M. Lopez, Dr. Hector P. Garcia, Dr. George I. Sanchez, John J. Herrera, and James De Anda, all of whom worked tirelessly with other Latino community members to improve educational opportunities for Mexican-descended students in Texas.[1] Despite their many efforts, frustrations, and actual accomplishments, most of the professionals who should make use of the stories of these Latino leaders, namely administrators and teachers in the southwestern United States, appear to have willfully ignored recommendations as well as research that highlight the education struggles encountered by all too many Latinos.

Most Americans today in fact are blithely unaware of the history to which I am about to refer. The reality and persistence of these issues, however, can be dramatically seen in the type of lawsuits that U.S. Latinos, much like blacks and other minorities, have been forced to file in attempts to secure equality of education in this country. Although educators have long monitored progress on a great number of education issues, they have largely remained aware of but impassively oblivious to the struggles that Mexican-descent students encounter. It is only by resorting reluctantly to the courts that Latinos have been able to improve their education prospects.

The primary historian who has traced the efforts of the Mexican American community to educate its offspring is Guadalupe San Miguel. San Miguel, for example, once itemized twenty-eight court cases where Latinos, frustrated by the inaction of school districts and education officials, filed lawsuits to secure equal schooling opportunities.[2] Four of the twenty-eight lawsuits filed by Latino plaintiffs went to court years before *Brown* in 1954. These were *Independent School District v. Salvatierra* (San Antonio, 1930); *Ramirez v. State* (Texas, 1931); *Mendez et al. v. Westminster School District of Orange County et al.* (California, 1947); and *Delgado et al. v. Bastrop Independent School District* (Texas, 1948). Another case, *Hernandez v. Texas,* was filed the same year that the Supreme Court made the decision to desegregate public schools. It was only *after* the Supreme Court *Brown* decision of 1954, though, that the other twenty-three lawsuits were filed. This fact points out that Latinos were hardly on America's social radar then, even though Spanish-speaking people have been Americans since the Treaty of Guadalupe Hidalgo (1848) ceded from Mexico, New Mexico, Arizona, California, the southern parts of Nevada, Utah, and Colorado to the United States, and confirmed Texas as a U.S. state.

In 1930, Jesus Salvatierra and others filed *Independent School District v. Salvatierra,* alleging that this school district in Texas was practicing segregation by housing and teaching Spanish to Mexican-descent elementary children in the West End school building. The Anglo superintendent testified at length, saying, among other statements, that his "purpose in doing that was simply to instruct that group according to their own peculiar needs." He added:

> I was not actuated by any motive of segregation by reason of race or color in doing what I said I did. The whole proposition was from a standpoint of instruction and a fair opportunity of all children alike. That was the only consideration I had in the matter. There are decided peculiarities of children of Mexican or Spanish descent which can be better taken care of in those elementary grades by their being placed separately from the children of Anglo-Saxon parentage, because the average Spanish-speaking children know English as a foreign tongue, and consequently when you put him [*sic*] in a class with English-speaking children and teach him according to the method of teaching English-speaking children he is greatly handicapped, and we have that handicap extending clear up into high school in all content subjects, such as English and history, and where they come along together in the same grade we find again and again the children are handicapped because they are slow in reading English and read it with difficulty, and as a consequence fail in considerable numbers in English and history. Now, in mathematics they are very apt where the language difficulty does not obtain, and often make more progress than the American children.[3]

Educators of the time often sought to justify and to rationalize how they approached and taught Spanish-speaking students, believing that, aside from the language difficulties, these students were also morally inferior. The court, however, found for the defendants, and the decision included the clarification that the courts can directly interfere with school authorities, but "only when they go clearly beyond their administrative powers."

In the *Mendez et al. v. Westminster School District of Orange County et al.* (1947) case, Mendez and others complained that "they and all others of Mexican and Latin descent were being barred, precluded and denied attending and using and receiving the benefits and education furnished to other children, and are segregated in schools attended solely by children of Mexican and Latin descent." The Westminster defendants

Manuel de la Peña y Peña Presidente

interino de los Estados Unidos Mexicanos

A todos los que las presentes vieren salud:

Que en la Ciudad de Guadalupe Hidalgo se concluyó y firmó el dia dos de Febrero del presente año, un tratado de paz, amistad, límites y arreglo definitivo entre los Estados Unidos Mexicanos y los Estados Unidos de América, por medio de Plenipotenciarios de ambos Gobiernos autorizados debida y respectivamente para este efecto, cuyo tratado y su artículo adicional son en la forma y tenor siguiente:

En el nombre de Dios Todopoderoso:	In the name of Almighty God:
Los Estados-Unidos Mexicanos y los Estados-Unidos de América, animados de un sincero deseo de poner termino á las calamidades de la guerra que desgraciadamente existe entre ambas repúblicas, y de establecer sobre bases sólidas relaciones de paz y buena amistad, que procuren recíprocas ventajas á los ciudadanos de uno y otro país, y afiancen la concordia, armonía	The United-States of America and the United Mexican States, animated by a sincere desire to put an end to the calamities of the war which unhappily exists between the two republics, and to establish upon a solid basis relations of peace and friendship, which shall confer reciprocal benefits upon the citizens of both, and assure the concord, harmony, and mutual confidence

Treaty of Hidalgo

127

countered by saying the evidence showed that "children of Mexican descent had been and are being furnished with facilities fully equal to other schoolchildren." When the Westminster defendants lost, they appealed by arguing that the district court had no jurisdiction in the matter because no substantial federal question was at issue. The defendants then cited former Supreme Court cases where segregation was legalized under the "separate but equal" clause of *Plessy v. Ferguson* (1896) and similar cases. The appeals court, however, disagreed with the defendants, stating that the federal court had jurisdiction on the case because the school segregation was carried out by officers of the Department of Education in California. The court held that "nowhere in any California law is there a suggestion that any segregation can be made of children within one of the great races. Thus it is seen that there is a substantial difference in our case from those which have been decided by the Supreme Court." *Westminster v. Mendez* also established that the segregation of Mexican American children was illegal and not permitted, because Mexican Americans, the court held, were considered Caucasian.[4]

The landmark case that began to change educational opportunities for Latinos in Texas, however, was *Delgado et al. v. Bastrop Independent School District* in 1948. This lawsuit was filed by the League of United Latin American Citizens (LULAC), with Gustavo C. (Gus) Garcia serving as the plaintiffs' attorney. The main suit alleged that Mexican children were being segregated from the children of other white races in the absence of specific state law and in clear violation of the Texas attorney general's legal opinion. Judge Ben H. Rice of U.S. District Court in Texas agreed and ordered a stop to the segregation of Mexican-descent children. Until that time the public education of Latinos in Texas was abominable. The 1950 U.S. Census "showed that the median educational attainment for persons over twenty-five was 3.5 years for those with Spanish surnames and, by comparison, 10.3 years for other white Americans; about 27 percent of persons over twenty-five with Spanish surnames had received no schooling at all."[5]

Thus *Delgado* served as a precursor to how the Supreme Court would rule in *Brown v. Board of Education*. In addition, there were at least twenty-three more education lawsuits filed by Latino citizens between 1954 and 1981. The *Cisneros v. Corpus Christi Independent School District* case in 1970 established another benchmark case for Latinos. *Cisneros* held that Mexican Americans in a school district were "an identifiable ethnic-minority group" that had been segregated and discriminated against. Therefore, as in the case of blacks, they were entitled to all of the protections provided by *Brown*. This case confirmed once and for all that "segregation of any group of children, and not only Negroes, in public schools on the basis of their being of particular race, color, national origin, or of some readily identifiable ethnic-minority group, or class, deprives such children of the guarantees of the Fourteenth Amendment, even though the physical facilities and other tangible factors may be equal." The court went on to explain how to identify inequities when it stated: "In determining whether [a] particular school district is unconstitutionally maintaining [a] dual school system, the relevant determinations are which groups in the school district are underprivileged and politically and economically disadvantaged, and which, if any, of these groups are being unreasonably segregated in the district's schools." The court added that "desegregating" the schools by placing African American students with other disadvantaged Mexican American students was not desegregation at all. So long as disadvantaged groups were being segregated or kept from the advantaged group, then the unitary system called for by the law was not being achieved. In addition, the Cisneros decision required the school system to "assign Negro and Mexican-American teachers throughout the system on the same ratio that they are in the total teacher staff population and to take immediate steps to employ more Negro and Mexican American teachers."[6]

VOICES OF THE ERA

Julian Bond is currently the chairman of the Board of Directors of the NAACP. He also serves as a national commentator on civil rights and racial history. For many years he held a seat in the Georgia legislature but left politics after a run for Congress. Bond's father, Horace Mann Bond, was one of the group of distinguished researchers who supported the *Brown* legal teams with analyses of segregated education across the South. Bond's adult life has been focused on achieving equality for all Americans.

> When the 1954 decision was handed down, I was fourteen years old. I remember my father had done some research for the NAACP lawyers on the meaning of the Thirteenth Amendment. As it turned out, the Court didn't consider the evidence that he and others had gathered. But I remember the day of the decision as one of happiness and rejoicing. Something important had happened. Something strong had been said in defense of our interests and our rights, and the expectation was that great things would happen from it.
>
> From then to the present day, the meaning behind Brown has been shaped more by the opponents than by supporters. The NAACP immediately tried to recruit parents across the South who would apply for their children to go to these purportedly newly integrated schools. In some cases they had success. In some cases they were met with awful, awful treatment. It was the reaction of the white South that erected all of these barriers that in turn shaped the reaction of the black South.
>
> Prior to Brown, most communities that had an active NAACP chapter had a history of going to the school boards and asking for resources. The school boards gave them the least, if anything at all. They had a history of disappointment and the feeling that no matter what is asked for, it was never going to be given. They felt as though an equal education was not going to happen in their schools.
>
> As much as we loved and valued the schools, the teachers, the history, remembrances, equal education was never going to happen there. To get that to happen, we were going to have to sit next to their kids, because their kids were getting the best resources. The white schools were better only because the facilities were better, the books were newer, the buses that took the kids to school were better, and the playgrounds were better. It wasn't whiteness

that made them better, except in the sense that whiteness meant access to superior resources. The only way we were going to get equality was to get in that building with those children.

We sometimes have a romanticized view of the segregation era, but many of these schools were broken-down shacks. It was raining inside the classrooms, and many teachers did not have a bachelor's degree. Some classrooms had six grades in each room. No one can teach, no one can learn in those circumstances.

Young people today cannot imagine what segregation was like. They have no idea. Parents don't talk to them about it because they want to protect

Julian Bond

children from it. Some young people say they would not sit at the back of the bus, that they would have demanded their seat. But they don't understand that they would have been killed, too. It's so hard to convince young people of what that life was like. I have yet to find an effective way to tell my students, black and white, what segregation was really like. I can give examples. I can talk about how silly it was that black and white people didn't even play checkers together. I can talk about the difference between public school expenditures for black and white kids, give the facts and figures, but I can't show them what it really was like. I can't make the white kids stand in the back, facing the back of the room, or tell every student who comes in that they have to go in a particular door based on their race. I can't beat the ones who decide they won't walk through a particular door to show them that is what it really was like. It's hard to make them understand that experience now.

In 1950 the NAACP was the civil rights organization. There was no Southern Christian Leadership Conference. There was barely any Congress of Racial Equality. There was no Student Nonviolent Coordinating Committee. Although various towns and cities across the country had their own local civil rights groups, the NAACP was organized nationwide. It had branches in every state and members everywhere. It was natural that the NAACP would initiate the major desegregation case; it had experience doing this as a grassroots network. Now, the NAACP while still the biggest, is only one of numerous civil rights organizations.

The NAACP's current goals for public school education concern the overconcentration of minority students in failing schools. We have asked the governors and the education officials in each of the fifty states to sign on to our plan for improving education. Our plan says very little about integration or segregation. Instead, it is about ensuring that each of the schools is equal to the next one. So far thirty states have agreed, and we are monitoring their progress. Some are trying and some are not doing much at all. On the one hand, the NAACP is still worried about the Brown mandate, but on the other hand, we are doing our part to try to fix the situation as it exists right now. Today, Hispanic children in Los Angeles are more rigidly racially segregated than black children in Mississippi. Although black children in Mississippi aren't widely integrated, it is astounding to see that the segregation index for Hispanic children is greater than that of black children in Mississippi. That tells us how great a battle we have yet to fight. The schools attended by racial minorities are typically at the lower end of the poverty line. These are horrible, horrible schools. We have big fights all over the country about school funding. The best legal efforts still have not been able to resolve the distribution of school funding such that every child within a particular state has an equal shot at an education. This battle just goes on and on. As soon as the progressive forces win one battle, the regressive forces find another hurdle. Fifty years does not compare to what might lie ahead.

The *Lau v. Nichols* Supreme Court decision of 1974 is the case that required school districts to provide students of Chinese ancestry instruction in their own language in order to learn English. Latino Spanish speakers, Vietnamese and other students held back by a school district's reluctance or refusal to provide such language instruction also were included. *Lau* held that "[a] school system's failure to provide English-language instruction [to a student] denied meaningful opportunity to participate in [the school's] public educational program in violation of [the] Civil Rights Act of 1964." The decision boosted bilingual education throughout the United States, helping thousands of English-language-deficient students who previously were not receiving the necessary language education they needed to succeed academically. In the 1977 case of *Rios v. Read,* the Court decided that a "school district receiving federal funds is required to develop effective programs to assure as much as is reasonably possible a language-deficient child's growth in English language and it is not enough simply to provide program[s] for language-deficient children or even to staff the program with bilingual teachers."

Some of these Latino lawsuits, however, were dismissed. For example, *Alvarado v. El Paso Independent School District* in 1971 was a class action case filed by parents in the El Paso Independent School District seeking "relief from alleged racial and ethnic discrimination in [the] district's school system."[7] When the U.S. District Court dismissed the case, the plaintiffs appealed. The court ordered a "full and complete [public] hearing to determine if the school desegregation policies of the School District" complied with the *Swann v. Charlotte-Mecklenburg Board of Education* case (1971).[8] District judge Guinn claimed that the complaints of the plaintiffs were generalities that were not specific enough. The judge went on to say that private individuals cannot represent a class. The judge felt that the Alvarados should not have been allowed to file their lawsuit seeking to rectify alleged general allegations throughout the El Paso Independent School District because this is the duty and responsibility of the commissioner of education. Latinos, though, knew that the education commission showed little interest in their needs.

With the exception of *Independent School District v. Salvatierra* in 1930, only two other cases filed by Latinos were lost. *Zamora v. New Braunfels Independent School District* (1973) denied the plaintiffs relief from the existing segregation that Zamora alleged. Also, in *Otero v. Mesa Valley School District No. 51* (1974), Otero sought relief from the school district by seeking the establishment of a bilingual/bicultural education program. The court that reviewed the case, however, found no evidence of either segregation or wrongful hiring by the school district. Thus, if Latinos filed lawsuits, they had to be fairly certain that they could prove their claims and allegations because the courts traditionally scrutinized charges and required convincing proof from Latino groups that often were not familiar enough with the schools or the courts.

This short history of Latino litigation demonstrates that during the fifty-one-year period from 1930 to 1981, Spanish-speaking U.S. residents filed no fewer than twenty-eight lawsuits seeking relief from discrimination and asking for fair and equal educational opportunities. Many plaintiffs were able to show the courts that dual school systems existed. *Arvizu v. Waco Independent School District* (1973) and *Keyes v. School District No. 1, Denver, Colorado* (1975) are two such instances where the Latino plaintiffs were successful. In spite of such successes, after all these years, similar cases continue to emerge, each one alleging that Latinos receive educations that are unequal in terms of facilities, services, instruction, and resources compared with that of whites.[9] Clearly these lawsuits demonstrate a nationwide pattern of hindering and handicapping Latino education throughout most of the twentieth century.

OTHER LATINO EDUCATION LAWSUITS

Ramirez v. State (1931), *Cortez v. Carrizo Springs Independent School District* (1955), *Hernandez v. Driscoll Consolidated Independent School District* (1957), *Villarreal et al. v. Mathis Independent School District* (1957), *Chapa v. Odem Independent School District* (1967), *Perez v. Sonora Inde-*

pendent School District (1970), *Ross v. Eckels* (1970), *United States v. State of Texas* (1970), *Serrano et al. v. Ivy Baker Priest* (1971), *United States v. Austin Independent School District* (1971), *United States v. State of Texas* (1972), *Rodriguez et al. v. San Antonio Independent School District* (1973), *Serna v. Portales Municipal Schools* (1974), *Aspira of New York v. Board of Education of the City of New York* (1975), and *United States v. State of Texas* (1981).

If this sad history of the Latino struggle for equal education had not been ignored, the education conditions impacting Latino students would be considerably better today. What the record shows is that the number of Hispanic children who have been shortchanged by the schools since 1848 has been incalculable.

Ironically, many minorities also lead the efforts to abolish affirmative action under the belief that their educational achievements are depreciated, disparaged, and seen as less valuable. Yet almost everyone ought to recognize that race continues to make a difference in meeting the educational needs of students, and outlawing discrimination alone will not eliminate the effects of racial bias. The Supreme Court recently spoke very clearly in the *Grutter v. Bollinger et al.* decision of June 2003. Race matters both in academic and employment opportunities, it averred. Before the *Grutter* decision, the *Hopwood* (1996) opinion held complete legal sway in Texas. In *Hopwood* the all-white plaintiffs sued the University of Texas at Austin Law School for violating the Fourteenth Amendment and Title VI of the Civil Rights Act of 1964, claiming that the admissions procedures unfairly favored less-qualified black and Mexican American applicants. As a result, *Hopwood* shaped college admissions public policies in Texas from March 1996 until June 2003. During these seven years, the University of Texas at Austin, Texas A&M University, Rice, and other highly competitive higher education institutions struggled to admit enough minority students even though affirmative action was in effect years prior to the *Hopwood* ruling. The severe overreliance on merit, the default reality in the United States, made achieving even these low minority student enrollment goals very difficult. Beneficiaries of the status quo and the great majority of educators historically have demonstrated a marked reluctance to consider race as one of several factors that influence and shape their pedagogical approaches. Instead, the focus remains on teaching effectiveness and accountability concerns, yet neither of these issues centrally address the staggeringly high Latino and African American dropout rates. There is little agreement about the actual number of dropouts, though estimates in Texas range from as high as 47 percent to the single-digit numbers that are usually reported by the schools that reportedly have changed their data to cover up higher dropout rates. Throughout the spring of 2003, as many as two or three times a week, the *Houston Chronicle* carried a number of front-page stories that illustrated that several Texas school districts either do not keep records of dropouts or seriously undercount such students in order to secure higher academic rankings when they are evaluated. Due largely to the chosen indifference of educators, Mexican American and African American youngsters for this and other associated reasons are not yet achieving better results, and *Brown v. Board of Education* is now more than two generations old.

9

THE PSYCHE

The Dolls

The Doll Experiment of Mamie and Kenneth Clark is the best known part of the evidence before the Court in *Brown*. The experiment demonstrated that black children preferred white dolls to black, and was used to support the conclusion that segregation was "inherently unequal." Like any dose of strong medicine, however, the experiment has had a powerful side effect. It has fostered the notion that "race neutrality" is a civic virtue and that strong racial identification by black children is negative. Psychologists A. Wade Boykin and James M. Jones explain the strange consequences of this legendary evidence and the ideological fallout with which we are still dealing fifty years down the road.

—Tavis Smiley

The student-led strike at Robert Russa Moton High School paved the way for *Davis v. Prince Edward County, Virginia*. Aside from the small, overcrowded classrooms, Moton High School did not have a gym, a cafeteria, or an auditorium with laid seats, the very facilities that nearby all-white Farmville High School had.

The Psychological Evolution of Black Children's Education since *Brown*

A. WADE BOYKIN AND JAMES M. JONES

Among the many important legacies of the *Brown v. Topeka Board of Education* decision is the implication that racially separate educational facilities are psychologically detrimental to black children. The *Brown* decision established the idea that race consciousness was a risk factor in the psychological well-being of black children and helped turn this society's attention toward issues of social justice and the need to strive for greater educational equity and excellence for all children. The psychological principles underlying the *Brown* argument were fairly simple. The famous studies by Kenneth and Mamie Clark in 1947 showed that black children understood that they were black, but by the Clarks' account, valued being white more. Racial segregation had injurious psychological consequences for black children and black society. There are many critiques of this work and its implications, but what persists in the minds of Americans are the conclusions: black children suffered from lower self-esteem because of the stigma that accompanied racial segregation.

Social psychologists Kenneth Bancroft Clark and his wife, Mamie Phipps Clark, demonstrated that when children were given a black doll and a white doll and asked which one they preferred, most black children preferred the white doll. The children also attributed the more positive characteristics to the white doll. The NAACP Legal Defense Fund used this study to show the detrimental effects of racial exclusion and discrimination. The test results were submitted as part of the evidence used in the *Brown* case and were specifically cited in their ruling.

A subtle but powerful consequence of this line of argument was the notion that identification with one's race was associated with lowered psychological well-being. Race neutrality was viewed as an avenue for achieving racial equality. Removing race as a basis for judgment and decision making would somehow lessen the degrading correlates of race in the United States. However, we have learned over the past fifty years that the story is much more complex than that. Even as some Americans hold up the ideal of a color-blind society, research reveals that pejorative racial stereotyping and subconscious negative racial bias persist among white Americans. We have to be conscious of race to control and/or remedy its most pernicious effects. Race consciousness is awareness and understanding of the consequences, challenges, opportunities, restrictions, assets, and liabilities associated with racial group membership. It includes how much we are preoccupied with thinking about ourselves in racial terms; how much we factor racial group membership into our thoughts, actions, and decisions; and how much we perceive that other people relate to us on the basis of our race.

The implications of *Brown* should not be to remove race from our consideration, but to understand how it works and ameliorate its most pernicious effects while acknowledging its centrality in the drama of a multicultural and multiracial society.

Today, psychological well-being is increasingly associated with embracing and valuing social identities.[1] Research suggests that ethnic or racial identity may often be a source of elevated psychological well-being rather than the inevitable source of lowered self-esteem. Social psychological research suggests that at a psychological level ignoring race is like ignoring the elephant in the middle of the room; it matters, and it affects behavior whether we acknowledge it or not. People are still race-conscious in their basic psychological processes. They perceive racial differences, and either consciously or unconsciously, it influences judgments, emotions, and behaviors. For the most part, race matters in a negatively biasing way.[2] Race consciousness may be an effective way to combat the stigmatizing consequences of racial animosity and may build rather than tear down self-esteem. Demographics indicate that American interracial dynamics transcend simple black-white considerations. The June 19, 2003, edition of the *Washington Post* claims that Hispanics are the largest minority group in the United States. Many formal educational settings, even in inner city schools, are multiracial and multicultural. Moreover, the identity perspective from which black people interact with others cannot be simplistically captured in negative terms or in terms of low self-esteem, but often in terms of a positive sense of racial group identity.

The Value of Diversity Redefined

In spite of social psychological debate about the influences of race, racial disparities continue to exist in virtually every index of well-being. President Clinton's Council of Economic Advisers analyzed the economic and social well-being of Americans at the request of the Advisory Board of the President's Initiative on Race.[3] The council summarized their findings by noting that disparities between groups have persisted or, in some cases, widened, even though all racial and ethnic minority groups have experienced substantial improvements in well-being over the second half of the twentieth century. The report indicates that blacks, Hispanics, and Native Americans continue to suffer disadvantages in opportunity and in material and physical well-being. In spite of the *Brown* decision, the Civil Rights and Voting Rights Acts of 1964 and 1965, respectively, and advances in educational attainment, we still search for ways to reduce adverse racial disparities.

VOICES OF THE ERA

Zelma Henderson is the only living original plaintiff from the NAACP's thirteen-member roster in the *Brown* case. Now in her eighties, the former beauty salon owner has lived in Topeka since she graduated from high school in Oakley, Kansas.

> *It wasn't until my children were almost of school age that I realized that Topeka had separate schools. In Oakley, Kansas, where I finished high school, blacks and whites all went to school together. It disturbed me that the schools were different in Topeka. I lived on the east side of North Topeka, and the school my children went to was on the west side. I had to pass one or two white schools to get to the black school my children attended. My older son, who was only in first grade, had to catch a bus while I had to take the youngest one to kindergarten. I couldn't understand why black*

and white children were not going to school together like I had done in Oakley. I think it's very important for children to be exposed to all races; they learn to get along this way. It was my childhood experience that made me feel that integration could work in Topeka. I was just determined to help solve the problem.

I was a member of the NAACP when the case was pending. One of the attorneys asked me if I would be a plaintiff. I was glad to be involved because I didn't think it was right. With guidance from the NAACP attorneys, several parents went to the nearest white school to enroll their children. All of them were denied. It was this refusal to admit our children that actually started the suit. There were a lot of people who were saying that if we followed through with this case then we would be fired or wouldn't be able to get other jobs. Many organizations did not want to be plaintiffs because they feared that they would also lose their jobs if they testified. In fact, even Oliver Brown, who the case is named after, didn't want to testify at first because he was afraid of losing his job at the Santa Fe Railroad Company.

I remember going to the attorney's office for a practice session. They asked us questions that they thought the other attorneys would ask us on the stand. Bob Carter remarked that I was superb because I always remained focused. I was like my father, very forward and straight and determined.

I became involved because I thought that right was right! Lit-

Zelma Henderson

tle children shouldn't be given a guilt complex or made to feel that they weren't good enough to attend certain schools. I wanted desegregation! And I figured the rest would take care of itself.

After fifty years I still think more good came out of the case than bad. I know the decision helped to open up many a field for us. I know Topeka has been very lax in supporting Brown, *and it hasn't been very effective in enforcing the decision. But at elementary schools the children play together. I see them going hand in hand, little black ones, little white ones. Seeing them play together makes me feel very good, and I know that this is the way it is supposed to be. Although I know there is some unfinished business, I can more readily see the good that has come from this case.*

I would like to be remembered as someone who believed in what was right. I was someone who was willing to go to the law in order to help right something that was very wrong. I do not believe in fighting though; I practice love because love begets love. But some of the reactions in the country to integration made me feel sad. It sickened my heart but I still believe like Dr. King believed, we can fight the peaceful way.

Central to any goal of enhancing equity and excellence in a multiracial and multicultural society is the recognition that "diversity" is a potential asset for academic learning. There are two types of diversity: vertical and horizontal.

Many conceive of diversity as a vertical concept, where variations among people are linked to membership in racial or ethnic groups, and their differences are associated with deficits, inadequacies, or deficiencies, either inherited or acquired. This concept of diversity is applied to educational settings and used to explain the relatively poor performance of minority group members. Vertical diversity is the pessimistic definition of diversity, akin to views that fueled racial segregation—that minority group students are born inferior and thus will always be so, that they cannot benefit from a quality education and would certainly drag down educational outcomes of majority group students. The more liberal side of this view is that minority group students have background deficits tied to inadequate life experiences that are not as good as others and that must be overcome or compensated for if they are to be academically successful. Both of these viewpoints portray diversity in vertical terms. But this does not have to be the case.

A horizontal approach to diversity conveys variations among people and differences in experience as simply different, without attaching values to them. None is inadequate or deficient or lacking. Every group and most every experience has value. Horizontal diversity holds that people from diverse backgrounds all have qualities from their experiences that are worthwhile, potentially of value, and can be affirmed.

Vertical diversity in educational models leads to stratification of children on the basis of academic criteria such as reading level, test performance, presumed ability, family dynamics, prior life experiences, or basic abilities. Vertical views of diversity are outcome-dependent and summarize performance or justify differential outcomes.

Horizontal diversity, by contrast, treats children on the basis of individual, social, and cultural antecedents such as learning preferences, family dynamics, cultural interests, values, and prior experiences, and informs pedagogical processes that incorporate these antecedents as means to positively influence learning. It is process-dependent and justifies that educational excellence and equity are not contingent on sameness of expression. Diversity in this sense emphasizes an integration of multiple resources and experiences that help formulate instructional approaches that challenge the status quo. This leads to more educational opportunities for a wider population. As such, education truly becomes a vehicle for attaining social justice.

We link the concept of horizontal diversity to psychosocial integrity, which means that experiences and attributes should be understood as they are perceived by those who live them. By their very existence, all experience and being have value and integrity and should be understood on their own terms and not judged from a "mainstream" perspective. Psychosocial integrity takes as a given that human beings, regardless of background, strive to attach meaning to their lives, make sense of their lives and their experiences, and optimize their lives according to the meanings they attach to existence. They do so because they are human and, all in their own way, affirm their humanity.

Horizontal diversity in education is based on the concept of psychosocial integrity, with integrity understood as existing in an integrated whole, in all its multiple facets.[4] The concept of psychosocial integrity is a balanced consideration of strengths and weaknesses, positives and negatives, uniformities and inconsistencies, and similarities and dissimilarities within a group as well as in relation to other groups. The goal is to understand the targeted populations on their own terms and how they make sense of their lives in a constantly changing environment. Focusing on integrity creates greater learning opportunities and schooling outcomes for all children, particularly for African American, Latino and other educationally disenfranchised children. Integrity conveys that there is complexity, coherence, and texture in people's life experiences and it exists in the experiences of people from diverse backgrounds, even among those whose experiences diverge from a mainstream middle-class standard.[5]

This approach seeks to glean from students' everyday lives and experiences, potentials and ways of functioning that can be fashioned into assets to be capitalized on in school settings to achieve greater academic outcomes.

Contemporary Approaches to Schooling Black Children

It has been long established that African American and other children of color fare poorly in our nation's public schools. Many have called for school reform, but often efforts have been scattershot and did not pay heed, in constructive ways, to the actual lived experiences of black and other minority group children.

With these observations in mind, in 1999, the first author and his colleagues at Howard University's Center for Research on the Education of Students Placed at Risk formulated the Talent Quest model of school reform. This model was designed to provide multiple school improvement programs, interventions, and strategies covering the full range of schooling activities, all coordinated around a common set of principles and with a common philosophy of education. Incorporated centrally into the philosophy and corresponding principles is the notion that all children can learn to high standards as long as the school environment is set up to be sufficiently supportive of such an outcome. There is an insistent focus on building on the assets that students and other stakeholders bring with them into the schooling environment. Talent Quest implements (1) professional development for teachers; (2) leadership support for administrators; (3) frameworks for classroom management, language arts, and mathematics; (4) in-school tutorial and after-school skill reinforcement and acceleration programs; (5) social and cultural enrichment excursions for students and their parents; (6) school, family, and community partnership programs (parent workshops on their topics of interest, parent resources rooms at the school, and so forth); (7) enhanced student support services (e.g., counseling groups for behaviorally challenged students); and (8) assessment and evaluation support that (a) ensures that the various programs are well implemented; (b) discerns program outcomes; and (c) provides assessment data to guide instructional and other program interventions.

Our school reform work has centered in the Washington, D.C., metropolitan area, at elementary schools in low-income African American communities. To date we have accumulated promising results. Standardized test scores have for the most part steadily risen at our school sites. Teachers report greater effectiveness in delivering successful instruction. Teachers and parents both report noticeable positive differences in the attitudes and academic skills of children participating in our in-school tutorial and after-school academic support programs. Students enthusiastically look forward to participating in the academic support programs. Widespread tears were shed in one school when it was mistakenly announced on the school's PA system that the program would not be continued from the previous year. Parents' involvement in school activities has increased substantially.

One continuing challenge that concerned educators and educational researchers face is what aspects of diversity should be encouraged in public schooling. The preparation gap among many students from diverse backgrounds does not mean that these children do not have interests and skills that can be used to enhance their achievement in a formal educational environment. Capitalizing on the students' resources can lead to reducing differences in educational attainment among disparate domestic cultural groups while still raising the achievement levels of all students.

A reformulated educational paradigm requires improved schooling, instructional knowledge, and skills. Teachers and administrators must embrace the belief that virtually all students can acquire the school's valued outcomes providing they are given sufficient time, appropriate instruction, and support. This form of schooling also implies that professional development and ensuing instructional practice should be judged successful if they lead to improved performance of students, predicated on sustained improvement of educational practice.[6]

Integrity-based schooling activities positively capitalize on diverse student life experiences for pedagogical purposes.[7] Integrity-based schooling activities fall roughly into five interrelated yet distinct categories: (1) promoting meaningful learning; (2) teaching thinking and learning strategies while fostering critical thinking processes; (3) building a learning community; (4) utilizing cultural resources of students, families, and their communities; and (5) providing a supportive yet demanding learning environment.[8]

Meaningful learning conveys strategies that make connections among different topics, the students' personal experiences and future endeavors, prior knowledge, and to the larger world in which they live. This also involves coming to discern how to apply knowledge gained in school to a student's world outside of school, and in meaningful ways. Teaching learning and thinking strategies provides students with explicit tools and academic road maps that give room for constructive and focused engagement with relevant academic tasks. Learners are not viewed as passive. A premium is placed on active learning and on fostering critical thinking and other higher-order cognitive skills. In this regard curriculum enhancement tools such as graphic organizers are used.

In an integrity-based academic community, learning becomes an interdependent exercise where a premium is placed on collaboration and democratic participation. Students develop a sense of ownership in the learning process. A particularly noteworthy strategy is Numbered Heads Together.[9] Students in mixed-skill groups study together without knowing ahead of time which one the teacher is going to call on. Group members are prompted to ensure that all participants understand the material at hand. This method has proven to be particularly beneficial for African American students.

Langer documents that teachers who are successful by fostering test scores for low-income, primarily African American and Latino children that close achievement gaps with their white counterparts are ones who use strategies consistent with these first three integrity-based domains.[10] Teachers who integrate skills into the context of a larger, more purposeful activity; who make connections within lessons, across lessons, and between in-school and out-of-school experiences; who overtly teach enabling strategies such as planning, organization, and reflection; and who provide opportunities for students to work together in authentically collaborative ways that foster real intellectual exchanges are more likely to be ones who beat the odds.

With regard to the fourth integrity-based category, in addition, Ladson-Billings's work on culturally relevant pedagogy examines functional cultural resources[11] whose use in the classroom can lead to enhanced outcomes for black students.[12] She has demonstrated that those who successfully teach black children incorporate community-based issues and challenges that children and their families must confront and negotiate. Bell and Clark's research shows that when text material is punctuated with practices representing cultural themes traditionally associated with African American family and community experiences the outcome is greater reading comprehension and story recall for African American elementary school children.[13] These practices emphasize respect for eldership, flexibility in family roles, highly active and rhythmic games, and a focus on affective and social bonds. Interestingly, no effect on recall and comprehension was obtained as a function of the race of story characters. Furthermore, research also suggests that learning and performance conditions imbued with a communal theme (focus on mutuality, duty to one's group, and sharing as intrinsic ends), one that is historically associated with people of African descent, can lead to higher performance outcomes on a variety of tasks and cognitive demands.[14] In Lee's cultural modeling approach, teachers bring examples from African American popular culture into the class-room to practice critical thinking skills that can then be transferred to the formal curriculum.[15]

An environment that is supportive yet demanding is one where high expectations are set and where a focus on effort and improvement is pro-moted, along with a focus on sustained excellence. Project Seed has been a long-standing, successful enterprise for teaching advanced mathe-matics skills to inner city African American and Latino children.[16] Proj-ect Seed emphasizes constructive social relationships between its instructors and students and among students. Among other things, instructors convey high expectations to students by referring to them as young mathematicians and scientists. Instructors presume that there is no such thing as a bad answer, and strive to find grounds for encour-agement, if not merit, in every student's response. Instructors teach hand signals to students to display their support for each other's struggles with difficult material.

The Talent Quest model of school reform cited previously is replete with integrity-based activities. The literacy instruction involves response-writing exercises in which children relate the text to their personal expe-riences outside of school. Predictions and prediction evaluations are regular parts of the lesson framework. Graphic organizers are abundantly used in reading and math instruction. Whole class instruction is dis-couraged. Daily class meetings are held where students recite daily affir-mations reinforcing their high expectations and where they discuss classwide learning goals and the means to accomplish them. Teachers are prepared to focus on what prompts their students to respond well, on what their students' interests are, on where they are showing improve-ment, and on where they need more support and encouragement. Teach-ers also participate in one or more professional learning communities in language arts, math, and classroom management.

Recent research clearly suggests that using diversity to create more meaningful, culturally valued, inclusive, and collaborative educational experiences holds great promise for maximizing futures for America's children. Racially separate schooling does not automatically lead to damaged psyches for black children, and the diverse experiences of marginalized minority groups are not inherently negative or problematic. Deliberately focusing on concrete educational strategies that build on or that foster equally valuable or asset-laden experiences among racially diverse groups helps to create positive educational outcomes for our students. This is possible regardless of whether the setting is all-black or racially integrated and may even circumvent inherent racial biases and prejudices in educational settings.

Conclusion

Many changes in the education of black children have occurred since *Brown*. Without deliberate action, the educational plight of all too many black children will remain unabated. There is a persisting and troubling achievement gap now that seems resistant to change.[17] A great number from low- and moderate-income communities continue to go to racially isolated public schools that are all too often substandard in their human and material resources. Even though many black youths attend de facto racially integrated secondary schools, their educational experiences often remain profoundly segregated by race, with these differential experiences linked to lower academic outcomes.

Calls to reform public schools are arising from the White House, Capitol Hill, the business sector, and the educational community. This convergence speaks to the widespread belief that America will not meet its need for a highly skilled, technologically sophisticated labor force without the more successful education of children from groups that historically have had the most problematic educational outcomes. Fifty years after *Brown* we are armed with new insights that can help us to address these emergent and persistent educational challenges in ways that if not directly a result of the decision, at least capture its spirit, and will aid in completing the unfinished agenda.

10

RENEWING OUR COMMITMENT

A New Debate

Gary Orfield has been among the most exacting critics of the nation's failure to fulfill the hopes of the plaintiffs in *Brown.* He says, "The *Brown* decision undermined the legitimacy of Jim Crow and stimulated hope and protest, but mandated almost no change." Orfield has indicated that desegregation has proceeded at a snail's pace and the moderate changes that have come about were the result of the civil rights movement, buoyed by *Brown's* symbolic importance.

Orfield also criticizes the quality education movement's notion of "desegregating the money" and the Bush administration's emphasis on faulting teachers and students for educational failure while tinkering with vouchers. Orfield calls for a new *Brown v. Board of Education,* the meaning of which is fleshed out in his article.

—TAVIS SMILEY

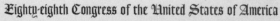

Eighty-eighth Congress of the United States of America

AT THE SECOND SESSION

Begun and held at the City of Washington on Tuesday, the seventh day of January, one thousand nine hundred and sixty-four

An Act

To enforce the constitutional right to vote, to confer jurisdiction upon the district courts of the United States to provide injunctive relief against discrimination in public accommodations, to authorize the Attorney General to institute suits to protect constitutional rights in public facilities and public education, to extend the Commission on Civil Rights, to prevent discrimination in federally assisted programs, to establish a Commission on Equal Employment Opportunity, and for other purposes.

Be it enacted by the Senate and House of Representatives of the United States of America in Congress assembled, That this Act may be cited as the "Civil Rights Act of 1964".

TITLE I—VOTING RIGHTS

SEC. 101. Section 2004 of the Revised Statutes (42 U.S.C. 1971), as amended by section 131 of the Civil Rights Act of 1957 (71 Stat. 637), and as further amended by section 601 of the Civil Rights Act of 1960 (74 Stat. 90), is further amended as follows:

(a) Insert "1" after "(a)" in subsection (a) and add at the end of subsection (a) the following new paragraphs:

"(2) No person acting under color of law shall—

"(A) in determining whether any individual is qualified under State law or laws to vote in any Federal election, apply any standard, practice, or procedure different from the standards, practices, or procedures applied under such law or laws to other individuals within the same county, parish, or similar political subdivision who have been found by State officials to be qualified to vote;

"(B) deny the right of any individual to vote in any Federal election because of an error or omission on any record or paper relating to any application, registration, or other act requisite to voting, if such error or omission is not material in determining whether such individual is qualified under State law to vote in such election; or

"(C) employ any literacy test as a qualification for voting in any Federal election unless (i) such test is administered to each individual and is conducted wholly in writing, and (ii) a certified copy of the test and of the answers given by the individual is furnished to him within twenty-five days of the submission of his request made within the period of time during which records and papers are required to be retained and preserved pursuant to title III of the Civil Rights Act of 1960 (42 U.S.C. 1974–74e; 74 Stat. 88) : *Provided, however,* That the Attorney General may enter into agreements with appropriate State or local authorities that preparation, conduct, and maintenance of such tests in accordance with the provisions of applicable State or local law, including such special provisions as are necessary in the preparation, conduct, and maintenance of such tests for persons who are blind or otherwise physically handicapped, meet the purposes of this subparagraph and constitute compliance therewith.

"(3) For purposes of this subsection—

"(A) the term 'vote' shall have the same meaning as in subsection (e) of this section;

"(B) the phrase 'literacy test' includes any test of the ability to read, write, understand, or interpret any matter."

(b) Insert immediately following the period at the end of the first sentence of subsection (c) the following new sentence: "If in any such proceeding literacy is a relevant fact there shall be a rebuttable

The Civil Rights Act of 1964

152

Brown Misunderstood

GARY ORFIELD

The fiftieth anniversary of *Brown* will produce what is probably the largest set of celebrations of a judicial decision in U.S. history. Since the United States is a country founded by lawyers and governed mostly by lawyers, a country with some of the most powerful courts in the world, it is fairly inevitable that we would exaggerate the importance of what courts do. It is not hard to understand why *Brown* will be so celebrated when we consider both the history of great progress on our hardest social problem and the memory of the nation's most progressive Supreme Court, the Warren Court of the 1950s and 1960s. It was such a beautiful story of social progress: this powerful Court, the institution that had helped trigger the Civil War by upholding slavery in *Dred Scott* and that had destroyed any hope for racial equality before the law by interpreting away the Reconstruction era amendments to the Constitution in *Plessy,* had in 1954 become the leading edge of progressive racial change.

Nine elderly white men solved the country's deepest social problem with a brief and sometimes eloquent decision. Before that there was apartheid; afterward the power of law began to remake the country. *Brown* was surely a significant event in what turned out to be the end of the system of official apartheid in the South after centuries of slavery and rigidly managed racial separation. It occurred at the beginning of a period of dramatic change that accomplished things that could not be achieved in the first 165 years of history under the Constitution or in the 182 years of colonization that preceded it. The South of the early twenty-first century is deeply different from the South of the midtwentieth century. *Brown* happened, and later the South changed. But was it really *Brown*?

During the midtwentieth century there developed a widespread belief among lawyers, journalists, and the public that the courts were and could be instruments for fundamental racial change in a society where there was almost always deadlock among the elected branches of government on issues of serious racial change. This was a period in which students eagerly poured into law schools to become the next heroic lawyers to challenge the entire social order on the basis of a brilliantly executed legal campaign.

In the celebrated theory, the great lawyers did their work, found their witnesses, faced danger and opposition with courage, succeeded in explaining very difficult issues to elderly judges from the political establishment who were convinced by the power of evidence and argument to order things that no elected officials had ever decided to do on their own. And the expectation was that the courts' decisions in these cases would be brave and wise. Young lawyers armed with logic and deep understanding of the facts and constitutional principles could appeal to a group of philosopher kings who could confer legitimacy and force major changes.

What could more perfectly symbolize this ideal than a Court unanimously deciding that the entire racial structure of seventeen states and the national capital violated the basic principles of "equal protection of the laws"? One day in May fifty years ago the Court did that. Apart from President Abraham Lincoln's issuance of the Emancipation Proclamation, it was the first branch of government ever to make such a sweeping proclamation. This one came, not in a time of war or great crisis, but in a time of peace and prosperity with no visible social movements and under a government that was the most conservative in two decades.

The images that are central to this fiftieth anniversary are of lawyers from the NAACP Legal Defense Fund walking into the Supreme Court and the black community across the nation celebrating when history turned. The basic assumption is that the decision somehow led to what was clearly a very important transformation in schools and in the society of the South.

In fact, the *Brown* decision undermined the legitimacy of Jim Crow and stimulated hope and protest but mandated almost no change. When President Kennedy sent his civil rights bill to Congress in 1963, 99 percent of black students were still in totally segregated schools, as were all black teachers; no white students were in black schools in the South. The basic idea was to let a very small number of black students transfer into white schools over a twelve-year period. The schools were almost totally segregated and deeply unequal. In the 1950s only about a fourth of black students were even graduating from any high school. The Court did not end apartheid, it only made it legitimate.

The decision by the Court, and the decision by President Eisenhower three years later to use federal troops in Little Rock, actually stimulated a stunning mobilization of segregationist political sentiment that swept across southern politics, creating what was in some ways the worst of all possible outcomes—strengthened segregationist political power based on fears of racial change and that produced almost no real desegregation.

What made the *Brown* decision effective in changing the South was the civil rights movement. This movement made race a matter of urgent national concern in the great confrontations in the South. Some pivotal moments include Martin Luther King's 1963 Birmingham struggle and the action of Lyndon Johnson, the U.S. Office of Education, and the Eighty-ninth Congress passing the 1964 Civil Rights Act and the Justice Department enforcing it. This law, together with the largest school aid program in U.S. history, used federal authority, a full set of sanctions, and big incentives to force change. Lyndon Johnson became the only president in U.S. history to show a real determination to cut off federal money from and to sue local officials who discriminated. It made the South the nation's most integrated region, in terms of schools, by 1970. It still was by 2000, though it is now going backward fast, and even as we celebrate *Brown*'s fiftieth birthday, it is imperative that we acknowledge that we are losing some of its most important accomplishments. There is no good substitute evident today for the goals that *Brown* put before the nation.

The civil rights movement and Johnson's Great Society might not have happened without the constitutional breakthrough of *Brown*, but without them, *Brown* would be remembered as a failure.

I participated in the August 1963 March on Washington when I was a student. My sign and many of the others carried in that march said, "March on Washington for Jobs and Freedom." The movement that came together in the mid-1960s had, as its aspiration, the goal of taking down all the racial barriers in society. The movement also aimed at making positive steps to redistribute economic opportunity, end discrimination, and provide training and support for those who were not prepared to take advantage of the new opportunities offered by the social changes.

VOICES OF THE ERA

Paul M. Gaston was a member of the University of Virginia History Department from 1957 to 1997, specializing in southern and civil rights history. An early civil rights activist, Gaston played an instrumental role in Virginia's integration movement. Gaston is a member of the NAACP; the Virginia Council on Human Relations; and the Southern Regional Council (SRC), an interracial southern organization that works to promote racial justice and educational equality for people of all races. He served as the SRC's president from 1984 to 1988. Dr. Gaston is currently working on two books. The first is his memoir about growing up in Fairhope Single Tax Colony in Alabama, founded by his grandfather, E. B. Gaston. The second is on the history of the civil rights movement.

> *I was twenty-six years old when the* Brown *decision was handed down. I was a second-year graduate student at the University of North Carolina. I was aware that there was a big civil rights movement coming and I knew I wanted to be part of it. At this time I decided to teach southern history at a southern university so I would be able to hold up a mirror to the people who would someday be southern leaders. I can remember really trying to influence my students in those classes in 1954 and 1955. Some of my most vivid memories are of students who told me how difficult it was going to be. It was tough to get them to understand that it would be through the* Brown *decision that things were going to change. I wanted them to see that you have to change the structure of society to change how people behave within it.*

In 1957 I began teaching at the University of Virginia. I imme-diately joined the NAACP and the Virginia Council on Human Relations. In 1958 I was elected to the executive committee of the NAACP. I had honorable views and a lot of knowledge as a south-ern historian, but I hadn't had hands-on experience. There weren't a lot of protests at that time, though we had a few bus boycotts. In 1963 I attended a sit-in and got beaten along with two black persons, William Johnson and Henry Ford Johnson. I became the central white person in that drama. I had already decided that I was going to use my professional position to contribute to the civil rights movement, so I knew my focus was going to be teaching southern history to southern people.

One of my most vivid experiences was traveling by car to Alexandria for the Court of Appeals hearings for the Charlottesville desegregation case. It was there that I learned an easy lesson. A judge ruled that the Charlottesville school board would have to admit black students. The school board would appeal the plan, it would go before a circuit court, and then we would have to travel to the circuit court to listen to these very learned people make their cases. I thought it was ridiculous that they were spending all this money, all of Charlottesville's money in court instead of in the com-munity. It is hard enough to integrate given all of the cultural differ-ences, the years of oppression, the fears, the lack of knowledge, and the stereotypes that people have. It would still be very hard even if everybody was in favor of integration. But instead of wanting to spend money for the leaders to make school integration work, all the leadership really was supposed to do was just spend Charlottesville's money by showing up in court. It was useless. People disagreed with me, though. In the university community there were relatively few activists, there were few people there who were going to march in the street or petition. Of course, there were those who would write letters, but I felt that by being an activist I would be involved in a community of people who cared to bring about change. Some whites disagreed with me vehemently, arguing that blacks should never have been admitted to the University of Virginia.

Paul Gaston

At that time I hadn't thought about the fact that the word "desegregation" didn't appear in the 1954 decision. I remember the famous Parker decision that stated that Brown did not require positive steps to integrate schools. This was interpreted to mean that after Brown you had to cease deny-ing admission based on a student's skin color. This is not the same thing as desegregating. I remember people debating the differ-ence in meaning between the two. Desegregation is the process by which we would stop segregation. Integration is the process by which we would positively bring people together. But I don't know if integration as a process had any real legal standing.

There was a big move in South Carolina led by conservative whites to avoid something like the Brown decision. They were try-ing to make separate seem equal. A lot of nice red brick schools were built in South Carolina, but by the early 1950s those kinds of actions came much too late. There never was a time in history when white people would take the proposition of "separate but equal" seriously. The "separate" part they understood. As for "equal," the effort never would have been made unless they were forced.

Clearly, the Brown decision has not solved this problem. But I do not think that the Brown decision created more problems than it solved. The enduring racial apathy of so many white people is at the heart of this, in addition to the failure of a community to see that the segregated school system is just one of the many prob-lems. There is a deep-seated opposition that has postponed for many years our progress toward a truly integrated society. In that society, maybe "one day people will be judged by the content of their character rather than the color of their skin." But we would do a lot better in terms of solving this complex problem if white people began judging by the content of someone's character.

When the Civil Rights Acts of 1964 and 1965 were passed, many white Americans believed that the civil rights movement was over and that all the problems were taken care of. However, Dr. King and others were arguing that the debris of segregation had only just begun to clear. The time was upon us to get to work. We needed to change the structure of society, to impact the architecture of American society.

From the writing of the Constitution to Brown v. Board *in 1954, this idea that all people were created equal was never a part of our fundamental American law. This fundamental law actually allowed us to do otherwise.* Brown *was the first major U.S. Supreme Court decision that provided simple justice and said that the law cannot be used to segregate anymore.* Brown *was monumental in that it made the Declaration of Independence and the Constitution come together. I can't think of any decision that the Supreme Court could make other than one that addressed the fundamental principles of the Declaration of Independence and the Constitution. If America is going to be what America claims to be, then the* Brown *decision is a major part of that struggle. We are a society that is based on the fundamental principles of justice and equality, and the* Brown *decision has pointed us in that direction more than anything else.*

People remember it as a much narrower movement because most of its objectives were defeated by the time President Nixon adopted his "southern strategy" to create a new southern-suburban-white ethnic coalition to dominate American politics. The Model Cities legislation was ended, and the gigantic 1968 Housing and Community Development law went on the ash heap. A great liberal accomplishment of the 1970s, the Humphrey-Hawkins employment legislation, was ignored, and national equalization of school funding was defeated by a single vote on the Supreme Court. Nixon appointed four justices, national child care legislation was vetoed, and the right of the poor to attain legal representation to challenge government policies was radically limited. The list goes on and on.

The problem was not a simpleminded desegregation-only vision, but an inability to enact and enforce most elements of the civil rights agenda. School desegregation lasted much longer because it was preserved by the courts until the first Bush administration finally won a clearly anti–civil rights majority on the Supreme Court in the late 1980s, which was further consolidated by the appointment of Clarence Thomas in 1991. The "equal" part of "separate but equal" was never enforced, and it is not being enforced as we resegregate our schools. I have asked desegregation critics in every part of the country, and no one has pointed to a single school district where white and nonwhite schools were segregated and equal.

People often say that we could solve the equality problem by "desegregating the money." This reflects a limited view of what makes a strong school. The problem with this line of thinking is easier to understand if we use a college as an example for analysis. A desirable college has a very well prepared student body and faculty, a good reputation, a range of academic programs, networks to future job opportunities, and further education possibilities. People understand that these are assets accumulated over long periods of time. No one would assume that simply putting a lot of money into a low-ranked college would immediately make it top-notch.

Brown turned out to be much more important as an idea than as a principle of law. The central idea of *Brown* was that the whole southern system of apartheid in the schools and all the other public institutions violated basic constitutional principles and was illegal. This severely eroded the legitimacy of the southern system and gave legitimacy to the black protest movement. Within a few years this erupted into one of the most important social movements in U.S. history. Equally important, the nation's majority political party adopted this basic principle of *Brown* and used its governmental power to force large changes before the opposition organized to begin dismantling the effort.

Brown v. Board was largely about the South, where most blacks have always lived and where the constitutional violations were apparent to one and all. It was never implemented with any seriousness outside the South, and the fate of other segregated minorities never received much attention. At the time of *Brown,* the problem was largely seen as how to get access for the one-eighth of the students who were African American to the better opportunities in the white schools attended by almost nine in ten nonminorities. About one-sixth of American students were in private schools, overwhelmingly white and largely Catholic.

The Court said nothing about the rights of Latinos until the 1973 *Keyes* decision in Denver, which concluded that Latinos, at least in the Southwest, had faced a history of discrimination equally serious as that of blacks and that these Latinos were entitled to desegregation remedies. In that very first case, however, the Latino plaintiffs pressed primarily for bilingual education. There was never a major effort, either public or private, to enforce the desegregation rights of Latinos, who became steadily more segregated ever since national enrollment statistics were first collected in the late 1960s—segregated more than blacks both from whites and from the middle class and increasingly facing linguistic segregation. Since a substantial majority of Latinos now live in states where affirmative action has ended, the consequences of attending inferior schools are even more serious for this community. By 2000, almost 40 percent of U.S. public school students were nonwhite, and six states, including the two largest, had substantial majorities of "minorities" in their schools.

In spite of a lack of any serious leadership from either the courts or the executive branch for school desegregation, the percentage of black students in predominantly white schools continued to rise until the late 1980s, perhaps because of the accelerating movement of the black middle class to the suburbs. Desegregation was durable.

The Supreme Court did not make the first of its major decisions reversing desegregation until *Board of Education of Oklahoma City v. Dowell* in 1991, and we are now almost thirteen years into a process of resegregation. Although we are nowhere near the segregation levels before *Brown,* almost all of the gains of the past thirty years for black students have been lost, and the South is going backward fastest.

School systems that have not had badly segregated inner city schools for many years are now seeing schools where virtually everyone is black or Latino and everyone is poor. Many of these newly segregated schools, often positively identified as "community schools" that were promised extra money and programs for a transition period, are now turning up at the top of the list of "failing" schools identified under the Bush administration's No Child Left Behind Act (2001). The basic theory of this act is that the fault for inferior performance rests on the students and teachers. Under this system, segregated schools are made "more equal" by taking money from them to allow parents to buy tutoring or offer students transfers, often to other weak, segregated schools, or by imposing more drastic remedies from state capitals. None of the various state takeovers of troubled school districts has ever ended racial inequality. Most have not produced any major gains in achievement, and normally the state throws up its hands and returns local control to the district.

The country is now rapidly undoing substantial parts of the progress achieved in *Brown,* even though things in the South are still far better for African American students than during the apartheid days. As this process goes on, it is very important that it be watched most carefully and that educators and politicians are held accountable for the results.

No evidence in public opinion polls reveals any significant turn away from our desegregation goals. Black public opinion polls and parents of students bused to integrated schools generally report strongly positive experiences. One example that comes to mind is of black parents in Boston who are engaging in voluntary desegregative transfers to the suburbs. Surveys show they are doing it for educational reasons, because they believe they are getting more educational benefits for their children, who will be better prepared for college and a multiracial life. And they are right.

What we need today is a new *Brown v. Board,* one that recognizes metropolitan inequality in schooling, housing, and job opportunities as a fundamental affront to any idea of social justice. We need to begin a new national debate like that which followed the *Brown* decision, and address issues of a much more profoundly diverse society in which 80 percent of the population lives in complex, interdependent, but deeply stratified metropolitan areas. We need to see if social movements and political change can revive and restore the accomplishments of *Brown.*

This may seem impossible but surely is no more impossible than the vision of Charles Hamilton Houston at Howard Law School that we could have a nonracist constitution. If separate but equal turns out in the early twenty-first century to be as fraudulent as it was in the first half of the twentieth century, a new movement will be needed to produce the kind of successful multiracial schools that can provide the base for a successful multiracial society.

REAFFIRMING THE LEGACY

CHERYL BROWN HENDERSON

Before the *Brown* decision, Topeka was a town with varying levels of integration. Some neighborhoods were integrated, as segregated housing was not as prevalent there. People really lived where they could afford to live. In this sense, Kansas was a perfect test case for school integration in the United States. The schools in Topeka before *Brown* were all built by the same person; four were African American schools and eighteen were white schools. They were all very nice brick buildings. *Brown* was not a facilities issue as much as it was an issue about freedom. Only the elementary schools in first-class cities defined as populations of 15,000 or more were segregated, while junior highs, high schools, and elementary schools in the small towns were not.

Oppression did not impact Topeka as it had in other parts of the country. We lived our lives in that protected cocoon of the African American community—our churches, our schools, our lodges, our social clubs, and our sororities. African American children didn't really notice that their lives were somehow thought of as being less important than those of white children. It was a positive experience.

After *Brown* that feeling of unity and cohesion was gone. One of my fondest memories is of going to NAACP meetings, and the adults and children would all stand to sing "Lift Every Voice and Sing." It was like being within this forest of adults. It made me feel very secure. To this day, when I hear that song, I get a warm feeling, the feeling of security because they were so determined. You could feel the determination in the room.

Life before *Brown* was not a bad experience because the adults made sure that we children could just be children. The adults understood that they needed to explain our value to us. We were loved, but also recognized that we had a responsibility to our race. We had home training. We understood what was expected of us. At the time we didn't understand that this expectation really was about the persistence of racism on a larger scale. All we knew was that there were certain achievements, there were certain milestones, and there were certain things we had to accomplish as African American children. Our parents placed a high value on formal education.

It was typical for African American men of my father's generation to fight against marginalization. He was always looking for places where he could use his leadership skills and his intellect. He was a boxer in the Golden Gloves. He thought he could use boxing as a means of not becoming marginalized. But he also had another calling, and I think he was very suited for the ministry. He went through the AME church training process to become a minister. Between boxing and the clergy, as an outlet for using those leadership skills, he was going to be known for something.

Charles Scott, a childhood friend of his and one of the attorneys in the Topeka case, personally asked my father to be a plaintiff. My father thought about it; this wasn't a snap decision for him. Dad was one of the last ones to join, and he was the only male in the NAACP's roster of thirteen adult plaintiffs. It was a compelling case for him, especially because the law didn't require segregated schools in Kansas. Topeka public schools could have always just chosen to integrate. There were schools two and three blocks away, some of the plaintiffs even lived across the street from them, but most African American children were being assigned to schools farther away. One of the plaintiffs' children had to make a thirty-three-block sojourn on a public bus to get to school.

During the four years leading up to the decision, from the fall of 1950 until May 1954, the plaintiffs lived their everyday lives. We didn't have a lot of direct involvement, and we weren't really a part of the strategy meetings that led up to the case. It wasn't until *Brown* was actually on the docket that my father became part of the process by having to testify in court. The only child to testify was Katherine Carver, as she was the oldest of the children in the plaintiffs' roster. The initial strategy was aimed at equalizing the facilities and making more resources available to us. It became more obvious to the legal team that there was reluctance by policymakers, politicians, and courts to implement even any semblance of better standards; the lawyers felt as though they had no choice but to fight for integration. I think the bigger picture emerged; fighting against this practice in public schools would have a much broader application. As Juan Williams demonstrates in his book about Thurgood Marshall, it was about access to resources. The resources were and remain where the white children are.

Kansas was unique in that it was the site of eleven school integration cases prior to *Brown.* So even before the national legal campaign, there were attorneys litigating those early cases in small towns where schools were illegally segregating. Kansas law stipulated that you could not segregate in the small towns. Our first case in Kansas was in 1881 in the small town of Ottawa, Kansas, outside of Orange, about forty miles away from Topeka. The eleven cases between 1881 and 1949 were all litigated by African American attorneys. Because Kansas had not been a state that allowed slavery, African Americans had this certain feeling of freedom that I believe fueled these changes, or at least caused them to pursue them. Finally when the Supreme Court used the Fourteenth Amendment to render its decision, *Brown v. Board* became important for every citizen, not just African Americans. It showed that we all had sovereign rights that could not be restricted by state and local governments. That decision impacted the lives of women, people with disabilities, blacks, whites, Hispanics, Asians, everyone in this country. Before the *Brown* decision we were still living in a system of states' rights, where some of our rights were honored and respected while some were not, depending on where you lived.

Oliver Brown

My father died in 1961, just seven years after *Brown,* so he didn't live long enough to even know that *Brown* would become the foundation on which so much else would rest with respect to civil rights and human rights. I just have to believe that he knows, because it's comforting, but I still wish that he were here to see the changes. It took courage to stand up, to be part of this group. One of the messages that we try to put out there for people to understand is that *Brown v. Board* is only named for my father. He was not the architect. He was a proud member of a group that took risks by taking a stand. We are no less proud of the legacy of having this case associated with our family name, but it is our personal responsibility that people understand that he was one of a few hundred who also stood up across this country. We also recognize that his gender played a huge role in the Topeka case being named for him.

The reaction after the decision came down was shocking. For example, the Southern Manifesto was written in 1957, and it was signed by white congressional representatives from southern states, people who were supposedly also representing African Americans. It was shocking to see how compelled they were to use any legal means at their disposal to overturn what the Supreme Court had done. My shock comes from the fact that whites felt so emboldened because of the privileges they enjoyed. They took to the streets with signs advocating for the Manifesto. They even pulled their children out of schools, as was the case with Ruby Bridges. They moved out of neighborhoods and opened private schools with federal money. That is shocking because African Americans have never enjoyed that kind of arrogance. Their behavior was born from the privileges that whites have gained on the backs of African Americans everywhere. I am sure they thought we had nerve to fight for integration, although they thought they had every right to take to the streets shouting expletives at African American students. I am not sure that some whites of that era even looked at our children as children. Instead, they saw African American students as the next generation in line to cater to them, so to speak. I think many whites just wanted to hold on to that piece of privilege, and they felt that *Brown* was part of chipping it away.

RUBY'S ONE-STUDENT CLASSROOM

Ruby Bridges was the sole African American child to attend William Frantz Elementary School in New Orleans after court-ordered desegregation in 1960. She was the first black child to enter an all-white school in the history of the American South. Federal marshals escorted six-year-old Ruby to school past angry crowds of protesters. The first year, the white parents pulled their children out of school to protest the integration. As a result, Ruby Bridges spent her first year in class by herself. Ruby's teacher, Barbara Henry, a white woman from Boston, was one of the few willing to teach a black child. Mrs. Henry and Ruby proceeded with the lesson plans as though there were no protesters or conflict outside of their one-student classroom. Now forty-eight years old, she started the Ruby Bridges Foundation, aimed at strengthening the parents' role in their children's education. Bridges tells her story in *Through My Eyes* (Scholastic, 1999).

Brown was significant in attacking the silence. Everyone had to start talking about race after the decision. It opened up a dialogue and forced the country to take on greater responsibility. In many ways, once the dialogue started, new problems were realized, especially as we began to understand the depth of racism. *Brown* helped to make it public; even after decades we are still facing the same issues.

There were many unanticipated legacies of *Brown*. The most obvious is white flight. Who could have anticipated that whites would start leaving communities because their schools were going to be integrated? Who would have anticipated that we would find ourselves with so few African American educators as role models when other doors opened?

Who would have thought that an academic achievement gap would be something that we would be talking about five decades later?

Prior to *Brown* our children were accepted as bright, capable children. They were in schools where expectations were high. They understood that they had to do their best, and they had goals and ambitions. Now we are facing a failure to meet even the most basic literacy skills. Now we understand the need for Afrocentric education, which would have been unanticipated prior to the decision. Thurgood Marshall, Charles Houston, or anyone else would never have imagined the magnet school. This concept was an outgrowth of *Brown*, and it is part of the unfinished agenda.

Policymakers are responsible for a lot. Among other things, they make certain that low-income housing is only located in particular sectors of the community. The ideas promoted in Murray and Hernstein's *The Bell Curve* have been in the fore since the 1800s. These ideas are supposedly grounded in science, while some use biblical teachings to try to reinforce the idea that blacks are supposed to be a subservient group. It is insidious when people want to suggest that there is some science that will justify their treatment of African Americans when in fact the achievement gap exists largely because those resources that Thurgood Marshall wanted access to are still not available to us.

This country generally knows how to educate children. Our leadership has not had the political will to make it happen. Every administration claims to have a new education agenda. From Eisenhower to Clinton to the current Bush administration, every four to eight years there's a new education agenda. How can any of it take hold when the next president leaves and his appointed secretary of education leaves with him? Then the next secretary brings his or her own agenda, and the cycle continues. It almost seems as though the position should not be appointed if we really want to make a change in education. Until we make a blanket statement and equalize this antiquated system of school finance, we are always going to have underfunded, poor, and failing schools. Our change should be renewing and continuing the promise of *Brown*.

TRANSCRIPT OF THE
BROWN V. BOARD OPINION

Supreme Court of the United States
Brown v. Board of Education,
347 U.S. 483 (1954) (USSC+)

Argued December 9, 1952
Reargued December 8, 1953
Decided May 17, 1954

APPEAL FROM THE UNITED STATES DISTRICT COURT
FOR THE DISTRICT OF KANSAS*

Syllabus

Segregation of white and Negro children in the public schools of a State
solely on the basis of race, pursuant to state laws permitting or requiring
such segregation, denies to Negro children the equal protection of the laws
guaranteed by the Fourteenth Amendment—even though the physical
facilities and other "tangible" factors of white and Negro schools may be
equal.

(a) The history of the Fourteenth Amendment is inconclusive as to its intended effect on public education.

(b) The question presented in these cases must be determined not on the basis of conditions existing when the Fourteenth Amendment was adopted, but in the light of the full development of public education and its present place in American life throughout the Nation.

(c) Where a State has undertaken to provide an opportunity for an education in its public schools, such an opportunity is a right which must be made available to all on equal terms.

(d) Segregation of children in public schools solely on the basis of race deprives children of the minority group of equal educational opportunities, even though the physical facilities and other "tangible" factors may be equal.

(e) The "separate but equal" doctrine adopted in *Plessy v. Ferguson,* 163 U.S. 537, has no place in the field of public education.

(f) The cases are restored to the docket for further argument on specified questions relating to the forms of the decrees.

Opinion

Mr. Chief Justice Warren delivered the opinion of the Court.

These cases come to us from the States of Kansas, South Carolina, Virginia, and Delaware. They are premised on different facts and different local conditions, but a common legal question justifies their consideration together in this consolidated opinion.

In each of the cases, minors of the Negro race, through their legal representatives, seek the aid of the courts in obtaining admission to the public schools of their community on a nonsegregated basis. In each instance, they had been denied admission to schools attended by white children under laws requiring or permitting segregation according to race. This segregation was alleged to deprive the plaintiffs of the equal protection of the laws under the Fourteenth Amendment. In each of the cases other than the Delaware case, a three-judge federal district court denied relief to the plaintiffs on the so-called "separate but equal" doctrine announced by this Court in *Plessy v. Ferguson,* 163 U.S. 537. Under that doctrine, equality of treatment is accorded when the races are provided substantially equal facilities, even though these facilities be separate. In the Delaware case, the Supreme Court of Delaware adhered to that doctrine, but ordered that the plaintiffs be admitted to the white schools because of their superiority to the Negro schools.

The plaintiffs contend that segregated public schools are not "equal" and cannot be made "equal," and that hence they are deprived of the equal protection of the laws. Because of the obvious importance of the question presented, the Court took jurisdiction. Argument was heard in the 1952 Term, and reargument was heard this Term on certain questions propounded by the Court.

Reargument was largely devoted to the circumstances surrounding the adoption of the Fourteenth Amendment in 1868. It covered exhaustively consideration of the Amendment in Congress, ratification by the states, then-existing practices in racial segregation, and the views of proponents and opponents of the Amendment. This discussion and our own investigation convince us that, although these sources cast some light, it is not enough to resolve the problem with which we are faced. At best, they are inconclusive. The most avid proponents of the post-War Amendments undoubtedly intended them to remove all legal distinctions among "all persons born or naturalized in the United States." Their opponents, just as certainly, were antagonistic to both the letter and the spirit of the Amendments and wished them to have the most limited effect. What others in Congress and the state legislatures had in mind cannot be determined with any degree of certainty.

An additional reason for the inconclusive nature of the Amendment's history with respect to segregated schools is the status of public education at that time. In the South, the movement toward free common schools, supported by general taxation, had not yet taken hold. Education of white children was largely in the hands of private groups. Education of Negroes was almost nonexistent, and practically all of the race were illiterate. In fact, any education of Negroes was forbidden by law in some states. Today, in contrast, many Negroes have achieved outstanding success in the arts and sciences, as well as in the business and professional world. It is true that public school education at the time of the Amendment had advanced further in the North, but the effect of the Amendment on Northern States was generally ignored in the congressional debates. Even in the North, the conditions of public education did not approximate those existing today. The curriculum was usually rudimentary; ungraded schools were common in rural areas; the school term was but three months a year in many states, and compulsory school attendance was virtually unknown. As a consequence, it is not surprising that there should be so little in the history of the Fourteenth Amendment relating to its intended effect on public education.

In the first cases in this Court construing the Fourteenth Amendment, decided shortly after its adoption, the Court interpreted it as proscribing all state-imposed discriminations against the Negro race. The doctrine of "separate but equal" did not make its appearance in this Court until 1896 in the case of *Plessy v. Ferguson,* supra, involving not education but transportation. American courts have since labored with the doctrine for over half a century. In this Court, there have been six cases involving the "separate but equal" doctrine in the field of public education. In *Cumming v. County Board of Education,* 175 U.S. 528, and *Gong Lum v. Rice,* 275 U.S. 78, the validity of the doctrine itself was not challenged. In more recent cases, all on the graduate school level, inequality was found in that specific benefits enjoyed by white students were denied to Negro students of the same educational qualifications. *Missouri ex rel. Gaines v. Canada,* 305 U.S. 337; *Sipuel v. Oklahoma,* 332 U.S. 631; *Sweatt v. Painter,* 339 U.S. 629; *McLaurin v. Oklahoma State Regents,* 339 U.S. 637. In none of these cases was it necessary to reexamine the doctrine to grant relief to the Negro plaintiff. And in *Sweatt v. Painter,* supra, the Court expressly reserved decision on the question whether *Plessy v. Ferguson* should be held inapplicable to public education.

In the instant cases, that question is directly presented. Here, unlike *Sweatt v. Painter,* there are findings below that the Negro and white schools involved have been equalized, or are being equalized, with respect to buildings, curricula, qualifications and salaries of teachers, and other "tangible" factors. Our decision, therefore, cannot turn on merely a comparison of these tangible factors in the Negro and white schools involved in each of the cases. We must look instead to the effect of segregation itself on public education.

In approaching this problem, we cannot turn the clock back to 1868, when the Amendment was adopted, or even to 1896, when *Plessy v. Ferguson* was written. We must consider public education in the light of its full development and its present place in American life throughout the Nation. Only in this way can it be determined if segregation in public schools deprives these plaintiffs of the equal protection of the laws.

Today, education is perhaps the most important function of state and local governments. Compulsory school attendance laws and the great expenditures for education both demonstrate our recognition of the importance of education to our democratic society. It is required in the perform-ance of our most basic public responsibilities, even service in the armed forces. It is the very foundation of good citizenship. Today it is a principal instrument in awakening the child to cultural values, in preparing him for later professional training, and in helping him to adjust normally to his environment. In these days, it is doubtful that any child may reasonably be expected to succeed in life if he is denied the opportunity of an education. Such an opportunity, where the state has undertaken to provide it, is a right which must be made available to all on equal terms.

We come then to the question presented: Does segregation of children in public schools solely on the basis of race, even though the physical facil-ities and other "tangible" factors may be equal, deprive the children of the minority group of equal educational opportunities? We believe that it does.

In *Sweatt v. Painter,* supra, in finding that a segregated law school for Negroes could not provide them equal educational opportunities, this Court relied in large part on "those qualities which are incapable of objec-tive measurement but which make for greatness in a law school." In *McLau-rin v. Oklahoma State Regents,* supra, the Court, in requiring that a Negro admitted to a white graduate school be treated like all other students, again resorted to intangible considerations: ". . . his ability to study, to engage in discussions and exchange views with other students, and, in general, to learn his profession." Such considerations apply with added force to children in grade and high schools. To separate them from others of similar age and qualifications solely because of their race generates a feeling of inferiority as to their status in the community that may affect their hearts and minds in a way unlikely ever to be undone. The effect of this separation on their educational opportunities was well stated by a finding in the Kansas case by a court which nevertheless felt compelled to rule against the Negro plain-tiffs:

Segregation of white and colored children in public schools has a detrimental effect upon the colored children. The impact is greater when it has the sanction of the law, for the policy of separating the races is usually interpreted as denoting the inferiority of the negro group. A sense of infe-riority affects the motivation of a child to learn. Segregation with the sanc-tion of law, therefore, has a tendency to [retard] the educational and mental development of negro children and to deprive them of some of the benefits they would receive in a racial[ly] integrated school system.

Whatever may have been the extent of psychological knowledge at the time of *Plessy v. Ferguson,* this finding is amply supported by modern authority. Any language in *Plessy v. Ferguson* contrary to this finding is rejected.

We conclude that, in the field of public education, the doctrine of "separate but equal" has no place. Separate educational facilities are inherently unequal. Therefore, we hold that the plaintiffs and others similarly situated for whom the actions have been brought are, by reason of the segregation complained of, deprived of the equal protection of the laws guaranteed by the Fourteenth Amendment. This disposition makes unnecessary any discussion whether such segregation also violates the Due Process Clause of the Fourteenth Amendment.

Because these are class actions, because of the wide applicability of this decision, and because of the great variety of local conditions, the formulation of decrees in these cases presents problems of considerable complexity. On reargument, the consideration of appropriate relief was necessarily subordinated to the primary question—the constitutionality of segregation in public education. We have now announced that such segregation is a denial of the equal protection of the laws. In order that we may have the full assistance of the parties in formulating decrees, the cases will be restored to the docket, and the parties are requested to present further argument on Questions 4 and 5 previously propounded by the Court for the reargument this Term The Attorney General of the United States is again invited to participate. The Attorneys General of the states requiring or permitting segregation in public education will also be permitted to appear as amici curiae upon request to do so by September 15, 1954, and submission of briefs by October 1, 1954.

It is so ordered.

*Together with No. 2, *Briggs et al. v. Elliott et al.,* on appeal from the United States District Court for the Eastern District of South Carolina, argued December 9–10, 1952, reargued December 7–8, 1953; No. 4, *Davis et al. v. County School Board of Prince Edward County, Virginia, et al.,* on appeal from the United States District Court for the Eastern District of Virginia, argued December 10, 1952, reargued December 7–8, 1953, and No. 10, *Gebhart et al. v. Belton et al.,* on certiorari to the Supreme Court of Delaware, argued December 11, 1952, reargued December 9, 1953.

NOTES

INTRODUCTION

Brown v. Board of Education: An Unfinished Agenda

1 Earl Warren, *The Memoirs of Chief Justice Earl Warren* (Lanham, Md.: Madison Books, 1977), 291.

2 Ibid.

3 Ibid.

4 Two academics have recently published books that bring the nexus between the civil rights struggle and the Cold War into the mainstream of American discourse: Thomas Borstelmann, *The Cold War and the Color Line* (Cambridge, Ma: Harvard University Press, 2001) and Mary L. Dudziak, *Cold War Civil Rights: Race and the Image of American Democracy* (Princeton, N.J.: Princeton University Press, 2000). As a starting point for an exploration of the earlier amnesia see Gerald Horne, *Black and Red: W. E. B. Du Bois and the Afro-American Response to the Cold War, 1944–1963* (Albany, N.Y.: State University of New York Press, 1986), 227. This is not the place to address the tradition of African American activists who have viewed the civil rights struggle in an international context except to recommend that the interested reader explore, as a Cold War example, the work of William L. Patterson who along with Paul Robeson and others presented a petition to the United Nations in 1951 charging the U.S. with genocide. (See William Paterson, ed., *We Charge Genocide* [New York: International Publishers, 1951, 1970].)

5 Brief for the United States as Amicus Curiae at 6. Eleven of the U.S. Amicus Brief's thirty-five pages are devoted to the foreign policy ramifications of de jure desegregation including a statement by the secretary of state that segregation causes "normally friendly peoples" to view the U.S. as "hypocritical" in claiming to be the "Champion of Democracy," Id. at 7.

6 Dudziak, 107.

7 Robeson spoke of the "Dixiecrats" of Mississippi whose "retaliation has gone well beyond threats." Paul Robeson, "Mississippi Today—History in the Making," *Freedom* (February 1955), reprinted in *Paul Robeson Speaks: Writings, Speeches, Interviews, 1918–1974,* Philip S. Foner, ed. (Larchmont, N.Y.: Bruner/Mazel, 1978), 395.

8 Stephen J. Whitfield, *A Death in the Delta: The Story of Emmett Till* (New York: Free Press, 1988), 36.

9 Higginbotham embraced the view of Judge Louis Pollack, who had offered this opinion, making exceptions only for the winning of the Civil War and the two World Wars. A. Leon Higginbotham Jr., *Shades of Freedom: Racial Politics and Presumptions of the American Legal Process* (Larchmont, N.Y.: Bruner/Mazel, 1996), xxxi.

CHAPTER 1

A Documentary History of *Brown*

1 *Plessy v. Ferguson,* 163 U.S. 537 (1896). *Plessy v. Ferguson,* judgment, decided May 18, 1886; Records of the Supreme Court of the United States, Record Group 267; *Plessy v. Ferguson,* 163, No. 15248, National Archives.

2 *Brown v. Board of Education of Topeka, Kansas,* 347 U.S. 483 (1954). Record Group 21, Records of the U.S. District Court of Kansas, National Archives—Central Plains Region, Kansas City, Mo. (hereinafter *Brown* or *Brown I*).

3 *Brown,* 347.

4 *Brown v. Board of Education of Topeka, Kansas,* 349 U.S. 294 (1955) (hereinafter *Brown II*).

5 *Brown II,* 349.

6 Ibid.

7 Ibid. Emphasis added.

8 A May 17, 1964, article in the *New York Times,* "Decade of Desegrega-

tion," stated, "A survey by the Southern Education Reporting Service indicates that only 34,110 of the South's 2,900,000 Negro pupils actually attended school with white children."

9 *Dred Scott v. Sandford,* No. 7—December Term, 1856. Judgment in the U.S. Supreme Court Case *Dred Scott v. John F. A. Sandford,* March 6, 1857; Case Files 1792–1995; Record Group 267; Records of the Supreme Court of the United States; National Archives.

10 *Dred Scott v. Sandford,* 1857.

11 *Dred Scott,* 1857.

12 Black Codes was a name given to laws passed by southern governments established during the presidency of Andrew Johnson. These laws imposed severe restrictions on freedmen and freedwomen, such as prohibiting their right to vote, forbidding them to sit on juries, and limiting their right to testify against white people, carry weapons in public places, and work in certain occupations.

13 The House Joint Resolution proposing the Fourteenth Amendment to the Constitution, June 16, 1866; Enrolled Acts and Resolutions of Congress, 1789–1999; General Records of the U.S. Government, Record Group 11, National Archives.

14 Slaughterhouse cases, 83 U.S. 36 (1873): "In 1869 the Louisiana legislature granted a twenty-five-year monopoly to a slaughterhouse concern in New Orleans for the stated purpose of protecting the people's health. Other slaughterhouse operators barred from their trade brought suit, principally on the ground that they had been deprived of their property without due process of law in violation of the Fourteenth Amendment. The U.S. Supreme Court, with Justice Samuel F. Miller rendering the majority decision, decided against the slaughterhouse operators, holding that the Fourteenth Amendment had to be considered in light of the original purpose of its framers: to guarantee the freedom of former black slaves. Although the amendment could not be construed to refer only to black slavery, its scope as originally planned did not include rights such as those in question. A distinction was drawn between United States and state citizenship, and it was held that the amendment did not intend to deprive the state of legal jurisdiction over the civil rights of its citizens. The restraint placed by the Louisiana legislators on the slaughterhouse operators was declared not to deprive them of their property without due process." *The Columbia Electronic Encyclopedia* (New York: Columbia University Press, 2000).

15 *Plessy,* 163.

16 *Plessy,* 163, Justice Harlan dissenting.

17 *Cumming v. County Board of Education of Richmond County, State of Georgia,* 175 U.S. 528 (1899).

18 Ibid.

19 *Gong Lum v. Rice,* 275 U.S. 78 (1927).

20 *Missouri ex. rel. Gaines v. Canada,* 305 U.S. 337 (1938).

21 *Briggs et al. v. Elliott et al.,* Civil Action No. 2657, 103 F. Supp. 920, Record Group 21, Records of the U.S. District Court for the Eastern District of South Carolina, Charleston Division. National Archives— Southeastern Region, East Point, Ga.

22 *McLaurin v. Oklahoma State Regents,* 339 U.S. 637 (1950).

23 *Davis et al. v. County School Board of Prince Edward County, Virginia, et al.,* Civil Action No. 1333, 103 F. Supp. 337. Record Group 21, Records of the District Courts of the United States, 1865–1991, National Archives, Mid-Atlantic Region, Center City, Pa.

24 *Gebhart et al. v. Belton et al., Gebhart et al. v. Bulah et al., Belton et al. v. Gebhart et al., Bulah et al. v. Gebhart et al.,* Civil Action No. 258, *Ethel Louise Belton v. Francis B. Gebhart,* and Civil Action No. 265, *Shirley Barbara Bulah v. Francis B. Gebhart,* 73 S. Ct. 213, 33 Del. Ch. 144; 91 A. 2d 137. Record Group 1225, Records of the Court of Chancery of the State of Delaware in and for New Castle County; Division of Historical and Cultural Affairs; Department of State Hall of Records, Dover, Del.

25 *Briggs v. Elliott,* 98 F. Supp. 529 (1951), Justice Waring dissenting.

26 Richard Kluger, *Simple Justice: The History of* Brown v. Board of Education *and Black America's Struggle for Equality* (New York: Alfred A. Knopf, 1976), 590–591.

27 Mary Frances Greene, *Teaching with Documents Lesson Plan: Documents Related to* Brown v. Board of Education, National Archives and Records Administration Web site, Digital Classroom: http://www.archives.gov/digital_classroom/lessons/brown_v_board_documents/brown_v_board.html, June 30, 2003.

28 Appellate jurisdiction: Case files of *Brown et al. v. Board of Education of Topeka et al.,* Nos. 1 to 5, October Term, 1954 (M1954, RG 267, 3 rolls). Roll 1: No. 1, October Term, 1954: *Oliver Brown et al. v. Board of Education of Topeka, Shawnee County, Kans., et al.;* Roll 2: No. 2, October Term, 1954: *Harry Briggs Jr. et al. v. R. W. Elliott et al.;* Roll 3: No. 3, October Term, 1954: *Dorothy E. Davis et al, v. County School Board of*

Prince Edward County, Va., et al.; No. 4, October Term, 1954: *Spottswood Thomas Bolling et al. v. C. Melvin Sharpe et al.* No. 5, October Term, 1954: Francis B. Gebhart et al. v. Ethel Louise Belton.

29 When requesting the original *Brown* records maintained by the National Archives and Records Administration, College Park, Md., the reference nomenclature for the original *Brown v. Board of Education* case files is as follows: *Brown v. Board of Ed.,* No. 1, October Term, 1954; *Briggs et al. v. Elliot et al.,* No. 2, October Term, 1954; *Davis et al. v. County School Board of Prince Edward County, Va.,* No. 3, October Term, 1954; *Bolling et al. v. Sharpe et al.,* No. 4, October Term, 1954; *Gebhart et al. v. Belton et al.,* No. 5, October Term, 1954. All were grouped under No. 1, October Term, 1954.

CHAPTER 2
The Attorneys

1 Genna Rae McNeil's insightful book *Groundwork: Charles Hamilton Houston and the Struggle for Civil Rights* (Philadelphia: University of Pennsylvania Press, 1983) provides an in-depth look at the mission of this great social engineer.

CHAPTER 3
The Legal Landscape

1 *Brown v. Board of Education of Topeka, Kansas,* 347 U.S. 483 (1954) (hereinafter *Brown* or *Brown I*); and *Brown v. Board of Education of Topeka, Kansas,* 349 U.S. 294 (1955) (hereinafter *Brown II*).

2 U.S. Declaration of Independence.

3 See U.S. Constitution, Thirteenth and Fourteenth Amendments.

4 *Brown II,* 349 U.S. at 301.

5 See *Cooper v. Aaron,* 358 U.S. 1 (1958).

6 *Morgan v. Hennigan,* 379 F. Supp. 410, 424 (D. Mass. 1974) (ordering busing to integrate Boston public school system).

7 515 U.S. 70 (1995).

8 Ibid.

9 *Korematsu v. United States,* 323 U.S. 214 (1944).

10 Randall L. Kennedy, "*McClesky v. Kemp:* Race, Capital Punishment, and the Supreme Court," *Harvard Law Review* 101 (1988): 1388–1418.

11 *Brown I,* 347 U.S. at 495, n. 11 (citing studies showing the effect of racial prejudice on personality development).

12 Kennedy, 1417.

13 Kennedy, 1417–1418.

14 Kennedy, 1418.

15 Abraham Lincoln, Second Inaugural Address, 1865. *Great Speeches* with notes by John Grafton. (1991) (New York: Dover Publications, 1991), p.107.

16 Ibid. For a more detailed discussion of the relations among Lincoln, atonement, and nationhood see Eric J. Miller, "Reconceiving Reparations: Multiple Strategies in the Reparations Debate," *Third World Law Journal* 23 (forthcoming 2003).

17 305 U.S. 337 (1938).

18 339 U.S. 629 (1950).

19 339 U.S. 637 (1950).

20 *Briggs v. Elliot,* 132 F. Supp. 776 (E.D.S.C., 1955)

21 *Briggs v. Elliot* at 777; see also Patterson, *supra* n. 3, at 85.

22 *Briggs,* 132 F. Supp. at 777–778.

23 Carl Tobias, "Public School Desegregation in Virginia during the Post-*Brown* Decade," *William & Mary Law Review* 37 (1996): 1269.

24 Peltason, Jack W. *Fifty-Eight Lonely Men: Southern Federal Judges and School Desegregation.* New York: Harcourt, Brace, 1961.

25 White, *supra* note 18.

26 Tobias, 1269.

27 Ibid.

28 See White, *supra* n. 18.

29 Tobias, 1269.

30 Gary Orfield and Susan Eaton, *Dismantling Desegregation: The Quiet Reversal of* Brown v. Board of Education (New York: New Press, 1996), 7–8.

31 Ibid.

32 Tobias, 1261.

33 Orfield and Eaton, 482–483.

34 *New York Times,* September 20, 1975.

35 Ibid.

36 Brian J. Sheehan, *The Boston School Integration Dispute: Social Change and Legal Maneuvers* (New York: Columbia University Press, 1984).

37 *New York Times,* January 9, 1975.

38 *New York Times,* December 11, 1975.

39 *Boston Globe,* December 12, 1974, sec. 4, 28

40 Sheehan, 248.

41 *Newsweek,* September 15, 1975.

42 *Keyes v. Denver,* 413 U.S. 189, 208. ("We emphasize that the differentiating factor between de jure segregation and so-called de facto segregation to which we referred in *Swann* is purpose or intent to segregate.")

43 Chief Justice Warren Burger broadened the Court's definition of de facto segregation so that amalgamations of de jure and de facto segregation would be unconstitutional. Doctrinally, this means that to violate the equal-protection clause there must be some purposeful intent to segregate.

44 *Swann v. Board of Education,* 402 U.S. 1 (1971), 15. ("[A]bsent a finding of a constitutional violation, however, [efforts to have schools reflect their communities] would not be within the authority of a federal court.")

45 *Swann,* 402 U.S. at 422.

46 See *Board of Education of Oklahoma City v. Dowell,* 498 U.S. 111 (1991) (Chief Justice Rehnquist writing); *Swann,* 402 U.S. at 422.

47 *Board of Education v. Dowell,* 498 U.S. 111 237 (1991).

48 See *Dayton Board of Education v. Brinkman,* 433 U.S. 406, 413 (1979) ("The finding that the pupil population in the various Dayton schools is not homogeneous, standing by itself, is not a violation of the Fourteenth Amendment in the absence of a showing that this condition resulted from intentionally segregative actions on the part of the board")(citing *Washington v. Davis,* 426 U.S. 229, 239 [1976]).

49 *Dowell,* 498 U.S. 237, 267 (1991) (Justice Marshall dissenting). (The majority's decision "risks subordination of the constitutional rights of Afro American children to the interest of school board autonomy," and that while "the courts must consider the value of local control . . . that factor primarily relates to the feasibility of a remedial measure . . . not whether the constitutional violation has been remedied.")

50 Ruby Bailey, "Colleges in Budget Squeeze; Crisis Hits Historically Black Schools as Lawsuits Threaten Affirmative Action," *Milwaukee Journal Sentinel,* March 9, 2003, sec. 7A.

51 *United States v. Fordice,* 505 U.S. 717 (1992).

52 *United States v. Fordice* at 733–35. The present admissions standards are not only traceable to the de jure system and were originally adopted for

a discriminatory purpose, but they also have present discriminatory effects.... It is not surprising then that Mississippi's universities remain predominantly identifiable by race.

53 *United States v. Fordice* at 748 (Justice Thomas concurring).

54 Ruby Bailey, "Colleges in Budget Squeeze." *Milwaukee Journal Sentinel* (March 9, 2003), 7A.

55 Ibid.

56 Orfield and Eaton, 6.

57 See *Freeman v. Pitts,* 112 S. Ct. 1430, 1443–1444 (1992) (stating that "the term 'unitary' is not a precise concept" and "does not have fixed meaning or content" and that while the concept of unitary status had been "helpful" in defining the scope of an appropriate remedy, it should not "confine the discretion and authority of the district courts").

58 *Missouri v. Jenkins,* 515 U.S. 70 (1995).

59 *Milliken v. Bradley,* 418 U.S. 717 (1974) at 718.

60 *Milliken v. Bradley,* 433 U.S. 267, 291 (1977).

61 *Brown v. Board of Education,* 98 F. Supp. 797, 797 (D. Ka., 1952).

62 *Brown,* 892 F. 2d at 856.

63 *Brown v. Board of Education,* 978 F. 2d 585, 587 (10th Cir., 1992).

64 *Brown v. Board of Education,* 892 F. 2d 851 (10th Cir., 1989).

65 *Brown v. Board of Education,* 892.

66 *Brown v. Board of Education,* 892 at 857–858.

67 Ibid.

68 Vincent Brydon, "District Names New Demographer," *Topeka Capital Journal,* February 5, 2001.

69 http://quickfacts.census.gov/qfd/states/20/20177.html.

CHAPTER 4
A Simple Dialogue

1 More on Geneva Crenshaw can be found in *And We Are Not Saved: The Elusive Quest for Racial Justice* (New York: Basic Books, 1987); *Faces at the Bottom of the Well: The Permanence of Racism in America* (New York: Basic Books, 1992); *Gospel Choirs: Psalms of Survival in an Alien Land Called Home* (New York: Basic Books, 1996); *Afrolantica Legacies* (Chicago: Third World Press, 1998).

2 *Giles v. Harris,* 189 U.S. 475, 488 (1903).

3 *Furman v. Georgia,* 408 U.S. 238 (1972).

4 *Gregg v. Georgia,* 428 U.S. 153 (1976).

5 *Roe v. Wade,* 410 U.S. 113 (1973).

6 *Planned Parenthood v. Casey,* 505 U.S. 833 (1992).

Chapter 5
The Teachers

People interviewed for this chapter include: Flora Chase, former chair, Business Education Department, Parker-Gray High School, Alexandria City public schools, Alexandria, Virginia; Melvin Futrell, assistant principal, Milwaukee Public Schools, Milwaukee, Wisconsin; Arnold Thurman, former head basketball coach, Parker-Gray High School, assistant principal, George Washington High School, Alexandria City public schools, Alexandria, Virginia; William Clark, chemistry teacher, Dunbar High School and E.C. Glass High School, Lynchburg, Virginia; and Elaine Chaffin Watson, business education teacher, Dunbar High School, Lynchburg, Virgina.

1 *Washington Post,* September 21, 1965.

2 Mark Howard, *An Historical Study of the Desegregation of the Alexandria, Virginia, City Public Schools, 1954–1973* (Washington, D.C.: George Washington University Press, 1976).

3 George W. Brooks, *History of The Tennessee Education Congress, 1923–1967* (Washington, D.C.: National Education Association, 1975); Thelma D. Perry, *History of the American Teachers Association* (Washington, D.C.: National Education Association, 1975); Vernon McDaniel, *History of the Teachers State Association of Texas* (Washington, D.C.: National Education Association, 1977); Gilbert L. Porter and Leedell W. Neyland, *History of the Florida State Teachers Association* (Washington, D.C.: National Education Association, 1977); and Jerome A. Gray, Joe L. Reed, and Norman W. Walton, *History of the Alabama State Teachers Association* (Washington, D.C.: National Education Association, 1987).

4 Thelma D. Perry (1975).

5 Richard E. Jones, "*Brown v. Board of Education:* Concluding Unfinished Business," *Washburn Law Journal* 39 (2000): 191.

6 Jerome A. Gray, Joe L. Reed, and Norman W. Walton, 156.

7 Ibid., 152.

8 Ibid.

9 Ibid.

10 Mary Hatwood Futrell, "The *Brown* Decision: Fifty Years Later."

11 Ibid.

12 Samuel B. Ethridge, "Impact of the 1954 *Brown v. Topeka Board of Education* Decision on Black Educators," *The Negro Educational Review* 30, no. 4 (1979).

13 *Education Digest* (Washington, D.C.: U.S. Department of Education, 2003).

14 *Patterns of Excellence: Perspectives on Diversity in Teaching and School Leadership* (Atlanta: Southern Education Foundation, 2001).

15 Currently 11 percent of the 83,790 principals in the nation are identified as minorities. It is projected that more than half of the nation's administrators will retire in the next ten years. The picture is even worse at the postsecondary level, where fewer than 5 percent of all higher-education faculty and administrators are minorities. *Education Digest* (Washington, D.C.: U.S. Department of Education, 2003).

CHAPTER 6
The Language

1 Teun van Dijk, *Racism in the Press* (London: Arnold, 1986), 4.

CHAPTER 7
Multicultural Impact I

1 "Naturalization Act, March 26, 1790," in Franklin Odo, ed., *The Columbia Documentary History of the Asian American Experience* (New York: Columbia University Press, 2002), 13–14.

2 Charles M. Wollenberg, "'Yellow Peril' in the Schools (I)," in Don T. Nakanishi and Tina Yamano Nishida, eds., *The Asian American Educational Experience* (New York: Routledge, 1995), 3 (hereinafter Wollenberg I).

3 "Petition from 1,300 Chinese Merchants for Schools, 1878," in Franklin Odo, ed., 49–50.

4 Wollenberg I, 9.

5 Charles M. Wollenberg, "'Yellow Peril' in the Schools (II)," in Don T. Nakanishi and Tina Yamano Nishida, eds., *The Asian American Educational Experience* (New York: Routledge, 1995), 13 (hereinafter Wollenberg II).

6 Wollenberg II, 26.

7 Wollenberg II, 24–27; Lane Ryo Hirabayashi, "The Impact of Incarcer-

ation on the Education of Nisei Schoolchildren," in Roger Daniels, Sandra C. Taylor and Harry H. L. Kitano, eds., *Japanese Americans: From Relocation to Redress* (Seattle: University of Washington Press, 1991), 44–51.

8   Ki-Taek Chun, "The Myth of Asian American Success and Its Educational Ramifications," and Bob. H. Suzuki, "Education and the Socialization of Asian Americans: A Revisionist Analysis of the 'Model Minority' Thesis," in Don T. Nakanishi and Tina Yamano Nishida, eds., *The Asian American Educational Experience* (New York: Routledge, 1995), 95–132.

9   *USA Today,* "2003 All-USA High School Academic Team," May 15, 2003, sec. D, 1–2 and 8–9.

10 Tessie Guillermo provides a list of Asian American ethnicities formally recognized by the U.S. government. They include (in order of population size based on the 1990 Census): Chinese, Filipino, Japanese, Asian Indian, Korean, Vietnamese, Laotian, Cambodian, Thai, Hmong, Pakistani, Indonesian, Malaysian, Bangladeshi, Sri Lankan, Burmese; in "Health Care Needs and Service Delivery for Asian and Pacific Islander Americans," in LEAP Asian Pacific American Public Policy Institute and UCLA Asian American Studies Center, *The State of Asian Pacific America: A Public Policy Report* and *Policy Issues to the Year 2000,* 64.

11 Shirley Hune and Kenyon S. Chan, "Special Focus: Asian Pacific American Demographic and Educational Trends," in D. Carter and R. Wilson, eds., *Minorities in Higher Education* 15 (Washington, D.C: American Council on Education, 1997), 46–48.

12 Valerie Ooka Pang, "Asian Pacific American Students: A Diverse and Complex Population," in James A. Banks, ed., *Handbook of Research on Multicultural Education* (New York: Macmillan, 1995), 418; Grace Kao and Marta Tienda, "Optimism and Achievement: The Educational Performance of Immigrant Youth," *Social Science Quarterly* 76, no. 2 (1995): 353; Morrison Wong, "The Education of Whites, Chinese, Filipinos, and Japanese Students: A Look at High School and Beyond," *Sociological Perspectives* 33, no. 3 (1990): 362.

13 Grace Kao, Marta Tienda, and Barbara Schneider, "Racial and Ethnic Variation in Academic Performance," *Research in Sociology of Education and Socialization* 11 (1996): 271.

14 Paul Ong, "The Affirmative Action Divide," in Paul Ong, ed., *Transforming Race Relations. The State of Asian Pacific America. A Public Policy*

Report IV (Los Angeles: LEAP Asia Pacific American Public Policy Institute and UCLA Asian American Studies Center, 2000), 324.

15 Ong, 326–328.

16 Hune and Chan, 53–54.

17 Jayjia Hsia, "Limits of Affirmative Action: Asian American Access to Higher Education," *Educational Policy* 2, no. 2 (1988): 119; Jayjia Hsia, *Asian Americans in Higher Education and at Work* (Hillsdale, N.J.: Lawrence Erlbaum, 1988), 165; Hune and Chan, 45; 54–55. For the latest comparative statistics on undergraduate degrees earned see *Black Issues in Higher Education,* special issue. "Top 100 Degree Producers, 2003. Part I: Undergraduate Degrees" 20, no. 8 (June 5, 2003).

18 Nathan Caplan, Marcella H. Choy, and John K. Whitmore, *Children of the Boat People. A Study of Educational Success* (Ann Arbor: University of Michigan Press, 1991).

19 Hune and Chan, 60; Wong, 357; Pang, 412–416.

20 Educational Testing Service, *Diversity among Asian American School Students* (Princeton: Policy Information Center, ETS, 1997), 8–10.

21 Margaret A. Gibson and John U. Ogbu, *Minority Status and Schooling. A Comparative Study of Immigrant and Involuntary Minorities* (New York: Garland, 1991); Stacey J. Lee, *Unraveling the "Model Minority" Stereotype: Listening to Asian American Youth* (New York: Teachers College Press, 1996), 31.

22 Stanley Sue and Sumi Okazaki, "Asian American Educational Achievements: A Phenomenon in Search of an Explanation," in Don T. Nakanishi and Tina Yamano Nishida, eds., *The Asian American Educational Experience* (New York: Routledge, 1995).

23 Grace Kao, "Educational Aspirations of Minority Youth," *American Journal of Education* 106 (1998): 349–384; Marta Tienda, "Optimism and Achievement: The Educational Performance of Immigrant Youth," *Social Science Quarterly* 76, no. 1 (1995): 1–19; and Marta Tienda and Barbara Schneider, "Racial and Ethnic Variation in Academic Performance," *Research in Sociology of Education and Socialization* 11 (1996): 263–297.

24 Ong, 325.

25 Hsia, "Limits of Affirmative Action," 119.

26 Laurence Steinberg, *Beyond the Classroom: Why School Reform Has Failed and What Parents Need to Do* (New York: Simon & Schuster, 1996), 92.

27 Sue and Okazaki, 137–140.

28 Don T. Nakanishi, "Asian Pacific Americans and Colleges and Universities," in James A. Banks, ed., *Handbook of Research on Multicultural Education* (New York: Macmillan, 1995), 688–692; Dana Y. Takagi, *The Retreat from Race: Asian American Admissions and Racial Politics* (New Brunswick, N.J: Rutgers University Press, 1992).

29 Patricia Gurin, E. L. Dey, Sylvia Hurtado, and G. Gurin, "Diversity and Higher Education: Theory and Impact on Educational Outcome," *Harvard Educational Review* 72, no. 3 (2002): 330–366.

30 Bill Ong Hing, "Asians without Blacks and Latinos in San Francisco: Missed Lessons of the Common Good," *Amerasia Journal* 27, no. 2 (2001): 19–29.

CHAPTER 8
Multicultural Impact II

I wish to thank Ms. Leigh Evans for helping me to retrieve a large portion of the information used to write this chapter, and Marie C. Portales, for her considerable help in securing critical information in this chapter.

1 *The Handbook of Texas Online* at http://www.tsha.utexas.edu/handbook/online, for example, offers a biography of Alfonso S. Perales written by Cynthia E. Orozco.

   Ezequiel Salinas served as LULAC president, and in 1939 he addressed a hundred school superintendents of Texas, urging them to eliminate racism and to correct distortions of Mexican Americans in the textbooks the students were reading. As of 2003, Mexican American historians and scholars are still seeking correct historical renditions of the contributions of Mexican Americans.

   Gustavo C. Garcia and Homero M. Lopez were two of the lawyers in the *Delgado v. Bastrop* 1948 case.

   Dr. Hector P. Garcia was a medical doctor and founder of the G.I. Forum in Corpus Christi in 1948.

   Dr. George I. Sanchez was a University of Texas educator and LULAC leader who testified, among many other accomplishments, before U.S. congressional committees on the state of Mexican American education.

   Moises Sandoval wrote a history of LULAC, *Our Legacy: The First Fifty Years* (Washington, D.C.: LULAC, 1979).

James De Anda was the Mexican American civil rights lawyer who participated in the *Hernandez v. Texas* Supreme Court case in 1954, and the attorney for José Cisneros in the 1970 *Cisneros v. Corpus Christi Independent School District* case. This case, educators should know, was the first that legally extended the Brown decision to Mexican Americans. *Cisneros* legally recognized Mexican Americans as an "identifiable [ethnic] minority group" that could be and frequently was discriminated against. Judge De Anda worked for the G.I. Forum, and he began a distinguished career by working for John J. Herrera (1910–1986), another early champion of Mexican American civil rights. James De Anda, former federal chief judge for the Southern District of Texas, was the second Mexican American to be named a federal district judge in U.S. history. As of August 2003 he was still practicing law in Houston, Texas.

John J. Herrera was the main lawyer, with Gustavo C. Garcia, in *Delgado v. Bastrop,* which declared segregation of Hispanics in public schools illegal in 1948. In *Pete Hernandez v. Texas,* John J. Herrera argued the first Hispanic civil rights case before the Supreme Court in 1954. For a full story on Herrera see Carole E. Christian's article on Herrera at http://www.tsha.utexas.edu/handbook/online/articles/view/hh/fhe63.html.

2 *"Let All of Them Take Heed": Mexican Americans and the Campaign for Educational Equality in Texas, 1910–1981* was published by the University of Texas Press in Austin in 1987. See pages 226–227 for a listing of the cases. It was reprinted by Texas A&M University Press in 2001. See also Guadalupe San Miguel's recent *Brown, Not White: School Integration and the Chicano Movement in Houston* (College Station: Texas A&M University Press, 2001). Previous scholarship on the issue is best articulated in Jorge C. Rangel and Carlos M. Alcala's "Project Report: De Jure Segregation of Chicanos in Texas Schools," *Harvard Civil Rights-Civil Liberties Law Review* 7, no. 2, (March 1972): 307–391.

3 Court of Civil Appeals of Texas, San Antonio, *Independent School District et al. v. Salvatierra et al.,* No. 8515, October 29, 1930. Rehearing denied December 24, 1930 (cited as 33 S.W. 2d 790). Appeal from District Court, Val Verde County; Joseph Jones, judge.

4 Mexican Americans regarded themselves as whites since LULAC, the League of Latin American Citizens, was founded in 1929. This identification indicated the pervasiveness and the virulence of the racism to

which darker-skinned people were subjected. The *Mendez* case in California in 1947 held that Mexican Americans were white, but in *Hernandez v. Texas* in 1954, the courts held that Mexican Americans were an ethnic community. In *Brown, Not White* (2001), Guadalupe San Miguel showed how being identified as whites was used against Mexican Americans to group such students with African Americans. Houston area education leaders then argued that the latter were being integrated with white students in the early 1970s.

5 See V. Carl Allsup's "*Delgado v. Bastrop* ISD," in The Handbook of Texas Online, http://www.tsha.utexas.edu/handbook/online/articles/view/DD/jrd1.html.

6 *José Cisneros et al. v. Corpus Christi Independent School District et al.,* Civ. A. No. 68-C-95, June 4, 1970 (cited as 324 F. Supp. 599).

7 *David and Dolores Alvardo et al., Plaintiffs-Appellants v. El Paso Independent School District et al., Defendants-Appellees.* No. 71-1555, June 16, 1971. Rehearing denied and rehearing en banc denied, July 14, 1971.

8 *Swann* allowed the courts broad powers when school authorities fail to implement feasible plans to eliminate segregation, and it identified "white" and "black" schools, providing for free transportation between these as necessary.

9 See, for example, "Race and Education Politics in Texas," one of two education-related postscripts in Marco Portales's *Crowding Out Latinos: Mexican Americans in the Public Consciousness* (Philadelphia: Temple University Press, 2000), 159–165. My wife, Rita, and I pursue the education of Latinos further in the forthcoming *Quality Education for Latinos: Print and Oral Skills for All Students, K–College,* which will be published by the University of Texas Press next year.

CHAPTER 9
The Psyche

Preparation of this chapter was supported by the Center for Research on the Education of Students Placed at Risk (CRESPAR), funded as a national research and development center by the Institute for Education Sciences (IES), U.S. Department of Education (R-117-D40005). The opinions expressed in this document do not necessarily reflect the position or policy of the IES, and no official endorsement should be inferred.

1 J. Crocker, B. Major, and C. Steele, "Social stigma," in D. Gilbert, S. T. Fiske, and G. Lindzey, eds., *Handbook of Social Psychology*, 4th ed. (New York: McGraw-Hill, 1998).

2 J. L. Eberhardt and S.T. Fiske, *Confronting Racism: The Problem and the Response* (Thousand Oaks, Calif.: Sage, 1998); J. M. Jones, *Prejudice and Racism*, 2nd ed. (New York: McGraw-Hill, 1997).

3 Council of Economic Advisers, *Changing America: Indicators of Social and Economic Well-being by Race and Hispanic Origin* (Washington, D.C.: U.S. Government Printing Office, 1998).

4 A.W. Boykin and B. Allen, "Beyond Deficits and Difference: Psychological Integrity in Developmental Research," in C. Yeakey, ed., *Edmund W. Gordon: Producing Knowledge, Pursuing Understanding* (Raleigh, N.C.: JAI Press, 2000), 15–34.

5 Integrity can be a source of assets that can be built upon in school settings. Complexity connotes that the experiences should not be understood in simplistic, stereotypical, or superficial ways, but instead in terms of multiple facets, variations, and depth. Coherence implies that the experiences make sense and fit together as they are interpreted from and help shape the frame of reference of those participating in them. Texture conveys that they not be understood singularly in terms of the absence of competencies, values, and behaviors that are characteristic of middle-class, mainstream experiences, or in terms of what is lacking by middle-class, mainstream standards, but by priorities, practices, and preferences to be understood on their own affirmative terms. Evidence supports that when knowledge of such potential assets is used to guide schooling practices, it can lead to enhanced outcomes for all students, and especially those from educationally disenfranchised groups. Further information on this can be found in R. Stanton-Salazar, "A Social Capital Framework for Understanding the Socialization of Racial Minority Children and Youths," *Harvard Educational Review* 67 (1997): 1–40; J. Langer, "Beating the Odds: Teaching Middle and High School Students to Read and Write Well," *American Educational Research Journal* 38 (2001): 837–880; A. W. Boykin and C. Bailey, "The Role of Cultural Factors in School-Relevant Cognitive Functioning: Synthesis of Findings on Cultural Contexts, Cultural Orientations, and Individual Differences" Tech. Rep. no. 42 (Baltimore, Md., and Washington, D.C.: Johns Hopkins University and Howard University, Center for Research on the Education of Students Placed at Risk, 2000); R. Tharp, P. Estrada,

S. Dalton and L. Yamauchi, *Teaching Transformed: Achieving Excellence, Fairness, Inclusion, and Harmony* (Boulder, Colo.: Westview, 2000); C. Lee, "Is October Brown Chinese? A Cultural Modeling Activity System for Underachieving Students," *American Educational Research Journal* 38 (2001): 97–141; C. Greenleaf, R. Schoenbach, C. Cziko, and F. Mueller, "Apprenticing Adolescent Readers to Academic Literacy," *Harvard Educational Review* 71 (2001): 79–129.

6 D. Sparks, "School Reform Requires a New Form of Staff Development," in S. Caldwell, ed., *Professional Development in Learning-Centered Schools* (Oxford, Ohio: National Staff Development Council, 1997), 2–11.

7 A. W. Boykin and B. Allen, "Cultural Integrity and Schooling Outcomes of African American Schoolchildren from Low-Income Backgrounds," in P. Pufall and R. Unsworth, eds., *How American Children Lead Their Lives* (New Brunswick, N.J.: Rutgers University Press, forthcoming).

8 Y. Bell and T. Clark, "Culturally Relevant Reading Material as Related to Comprehension and Recall in African American Children," *Journal of Black Psychology* 24 (1998); R. F. Ferguson, "Teachers' Perceptions and Expectations and the Black-White Test Score Gap," in C. Jencks and M. Phillips, eds., *The Black-White Test Score Gap* (Washington, D.C.: Brookings Institution, 1998), 273–317; A. Kaplan and M. Maehr, "Enhancing the Motivation of African American Students: An Achievement Goal Theory Perspective," *Journal of Negro Education* 68 (1999): 23–41; Langer, 2001; Lee, 2001; R. Marzano, D. Pickering, and J. Pollock, *Classroom Instruction That Works: Research-Based Strategies for Increasing Student Achievement* (Alexandria, Va.: ASCD, 2001); M. Pressley and V. Woloshyn, *Cognitive Strategy Instruction That Really Improves Children's Academic Performance,* 2nd. ed. (Cambridge, Mass.: Brookline Books, 1995); C. Tucker; R. Zayco, K. Herman, W. Reinke, M. Truillo, C. Carraway, and P. Ivery, "Teacher and Child Variables as Predictors of Academic Engagement among Low-Income African American Children," *Psychology in the Schools* 39 (2002): 477–488; B. Wasik and M. Bond, "Beyond the Pages of a Book: Interactive Book Reading and Language Development in Preschool Classrooms," *Journal of Educational Psychology* 93 (2001): 243–250; H. Waxman, Y. Padron, and K. Arnold, "Effective Instructional Practices for Students Placed at Risk of Academic Failure," in G. Borman, S. Stringfield, and R. Slavin, eds., *Title I: Compensatory Education at the Crossroads* (Mahwah, N.J.: LEA, 2001).

9 L. Maheady, B. Mallette, and G. Harper, "Accommodating Cultural, Linguistic, and Academic Diversity: Some Peer-Mediated Instructional Options," *Preventing School Failure* 36 (1991): 28–31; S. Kagan, "The Structural Approach to Cooperative Learning," Educational Leadership 47 (1990): 12–15.

10 Langer, 837–880.

11 Cultural resources refer to family, community, and peer-based experiences that give rise to funds of knowledge, and to practices that have local functional merit as people negotiate their everyday lives. Cultural resources refer as well to issues of popular culture and to diverse fundamental core values. These are at least three distinctly different yet certainly overlapping ways to conceive of culture. The first connotes cultural practices that are tied to changing functional or adaptive circumstances. The second has to do with expressive forms of culture tied to arts and to recreational and leisure-time activities. The third connotes the presence of enduring themes that are construed as salient or significant in the overarching beliefs and worldviews of an identifiable group.

12 G. Ladson-Billings, "The Power of Pedagogy: Does Teaching Matter?" in W. Watkins, J. Lewis, and V. Chou, eds., *Race and Education: The Roles of History and Society in Educating African American Students* (Boston: Allyn & Bacon, 2001), 73–88.

13 Y. Bell and T. Clark, 455–475.

14 A. W. Boykin, "Harvesting Culture and Talent: African American Children and School Reform," in R. Rossi, ed., *Schools and Students at Risk: Context and Framework for Positive Change* (New York: Teachers College Press, 1994), 116–138; A. W. Boykin and C. Bailey, 2000.

15 Lee, 97–141.

16 W. Webster, *The National Evaluation of Project Seed in Five School Districts* (Washington, D.C.: EDRS Report, 1998); H. Ebrahimi, "Seeds of Success," *American School Board Journal* 186 (1999): 50–52.

17 *Washington Post,* June 20, 2003.

CONTRIBUTORS

WILLIAM E. COX
Black Issues in Higher Education

 William E. Cox is the president and cofounder of Cox Matthews & Associates, Inc. (CMA), a firm specializing in publishing, satellite television production, training, and consulting, with offices in both Fairfax, Virginia, and New York City.

Dr. Cox also is president and managing editor of *Black Issues in Higher Education,* the award-winning national newsmagazine that has been serving higher education and the public since 1984. The company also publishes *Community College Week,* a national newspaper targeted for community, junior, and technical college professionals. Dr. Cox plays a critical role in the production of the award-winning *Black Issues* videoconference series, including the annual "Beyond the Dream: A Celebration of Black History" program.

CMA Consulting Group, a multiservice consulting firm, was added to the corporation in 1996. This branch provides assistance to institutions, organizations, agencies, and businesses interested in improving and extending the educational, career, and human development experiences of their constituencies. In 1999 Dr. Cox was responsible for the creation of *Black Issues Book Review,* the nation's only publication exclusively addressing books for, by, and about African Americans. This new periodical was recognized by the prestigious *Library Journal* as one of the "ten best new magazines of the year."

Among his other extensive administrative and organizational experiences, Dr. Cox has developed and conducted higher education programs for the U.S. Army and the U.S. Air Force, including the teaching of courses in the electronic guidance systems of sophisticated missiles at Redstone Arsenal in Alabama. His corporate experience includes tenure with the General Electric Company, where, among other assignments, he performed design work on the Apollo spacecraft ground support system.

A recognized authority on the development and delivery of adult education and counseling services to military personnel, Dr. Cox was formerly responsible for the worldwide network of U.S. Air Force counseling professionals. In that capacity he was responsible for air force counseling and testing programs and served as liaison to the Defense Activity for Nontraditional Education Services (DANTES). He holds the National Certified Counselor (NCC) credential of the National Board for Certified Counselors (NBCC).

His education credentials include a doctorate in higher education administration from George Washington University and master's degrees in both counseling psychology and public administration from Ball State University. He earned his undergraduate degree from Alabama A&M University. Bill also has taken both graduate and postgraduate courses at the College of William and Mary, Harvard University, and the University of Nevada–Las Vegas.

Dr. Cox has received numerous prestigious awards, including the following: he was named to the National Black College Alumni Hall of Fame (1994), received the Distinguished Leadership Award from the National Association for Equal Opportunity in Higher Education (March 1999), was inducted into the International Adult & Continuing Education Hall of Fame (October 1999) and the Gwendolyn Brooks International Literary Hall of Fame for Writers of African Descent (October 2000), and received the Alumni Leadership Award from the Thurgood Marshall Scholarship Fund (October 2000).

Among his numerous professional appointments, Dr. Cox is a member of the Board of Trustees of Excelsior College, the American Counseling Association Foundation Board, the Boost Alcohol Consciousness Concerning the Health of University Students (BACCHUS) Board, and the Advisory Boards of the Millennium Bank of Reston, Virginia, the National Council for Education and Human Development at George Washington University, Board of Regents of the University of Georgia System, and the University of the District of Columbia Business School. He also is a life member of both the NAACP and the Kappa Alpha Psi fraternity.

FRANK L. MATTHEWS
Black Issues in Higher Education

Frank L. Matthews is cofounder and publisher/editor in chief of *Black Issues in Higher Education*. He has devoted his entire professional career to black and minority concerns, primarily in the area of higher education.

Matthews also is a member of the faculty of George Mason University, where he has been affiliated for the past twenty-six years, teaching in both the Law School and the School of Business Administration. In July 1988 he was named senior scholar in the Center for Policy Studies in Education at George Mason University. In his position as assistant senior vice president and legal adviser for George Mason University, he was responsible for employment and regulatory matters that confronted the university during its period of rapid expansion.

Matthews has been active in many professional, civic, and scholarly organizations, including as past president of the American Business Law Association (Mid-Atlantic Region) and the National Association of College and University Attorneys. He sits or has sat on the boards of the Citizens Bank of Virginia, Resources for the Future, the Scholarship Fund of Alexandria, the Clemson University Honors College, and Blacks in Philanthropy, among other organizations. He was recently inducted into the Writers' Hall of Fame for his contributions in publishing.

He has conducted workshops, given lectures, and presented scholarly papers to many local, state, and national higher education, civic, and professional organizations.

In 1971, Matthews received the Bachelor of Arts degree in political science from Clemson University. He subsequently earned Juris Doctor and Master of Business Administration degrees from the University of South Carolina in 1976. During Clemson's centennial celebration, Matthews was named as one of their most distinguished alumni by the College of Liberal Arts and the Black Alumni Council.

JAMES A. ANDERSON
Consulting Editor

James A. Anderson is a leading researcher on the differences in student learning styles across culture, race, class, and gender, and how these styles interact with teaching styles in different classroom settings. Dr. Anderson is currently vice president and associate provost for institutional assessment and diversity as well as a professor in the Department of Psychology at Texas A&M University. Formerly the vice provost for undergraduate affairs and professor of counselor education at North Carolina State University, Dr. Anderson was responsible for planning and promoting an effective vision of undergraduate education there. He also supported faculty development, undergraduate research, assessment of student learning, and the general education experience and curriculum. Once professor of psychology and director of the Benjamin E. Mays Academy of Scholars at Indiana University of Pennsylvania, he held a joint faculty appointment in women's studies, and prior to that, was an associate professor of psychology and chairperson of the psychology department at Xavier University in New Orleans.

Dr. Anderson obtained a B.A. degree in psychology from Villanova University and a Ph.D. in psychology from Cornell University. He currently serves on the Board of Trustees at Villanova University. Selected as an American Council on Education Fellow and a Danforth Fellow, Dr. Anderson has presented keynote addresses at ninety major conferences and has conducted more than three hundred workshops at conferences, universities, colleges, and community colleges.

DARA N. BYRNE
Consulting Editor

Dara N. Byrne is an assistant professor at John Jay College of Criminal Justice of the City University of New York in the Department of Speech, Theatre, and Media Studies. Dr. Byrne holds a Ph.D. in rhetoric and intercultural communication from Howard University in Washington, D.C. She earned a B.A. Honours degree in English and sociology as well as an M.A. in English from Carleton University in Ottawa, Canada.

Dr. Byrne is a specialist in critical language studies, intercultural communication, and African Diaspora studies. She is committed to pursuing research that will positively impact black communities. Dr. Byrne is frequently invited as the guest speaker at community-based youth forums and training seminars. She was invited as the keynote speaker to Ottawa's first annual Youth Day Conference in 2002. She has conducted several workshops on topics such as social diversity, community mentoring, hip-hop culture in Canada, and health communication in the Caribbean.

Dr. Byrne has participated in several community-based health research projects. She was the recipient of the 2002–2003 Rockefeller Residency Fellowship at the Institute for Research on the African Diaspora in the Americas and the Caribbean (IRADAC) at the City University of New York. Among other things, the generous support of IRADAC allowed her to further her research on mental health beliefs and communication practices in the African Diaspora. Dr. Byrne has presented her research at several major conferences and research symposia in Canada, the Caribbean, and the United States.

Dr. Byrne also has extensive experience in online higher education. An avid researcher of online pedagogy, Dara has participated on thesis committees and taught research writing in the graduate liberal arts program at Excelsior College. She has also taught composition and communications courses at several other online institutions. In 2002, Dr. Byrne developed a diversity training program for online instructors and has led several seminars intended to improve the intercultural communication experience in online classrooms.

Dr. Byrne's current research project examines the portrayal of female criminal justice professionals in television and film.

DERRICK BELL

A civil rights activist and teacher, Derrick Bell is one of America's most celebrated and provocative legal scholars. Bell was Harvard University's first tenured African American law professor, yet despite his fifteen years of tenured service there, he gave up this prestigious position as an act of protest against the lack of minority and women faculty. He is currently on the faculty at New York University's School of Law.

His perseverance for racial equality and his determination to live an ethical life have been inspiring and exemplary to many. He is the best-selling author of *Faces at the Bottom of the Well* (Basic Books, 1992). Professor Bell has contributed his legal expertise and ethical convictions to an impressive list of other books, including *Ethical Ambition: Living a Life of Meaning and Worth* (Bloomsbury, 2002), *Afrolantica Legacies* (Third World Press 1997), *Constitutional Conflicts* (Anderson, 1997), *Race, Racism, and American Law,* 4th ed., (Aspen Law & Business, 2000),

And We Are Not Saved: The Elusive Quest for Racial Justice (Basic Books, 1987), *Confronting Authority: Reflections of an Ardent Protester* (Beacon Press, 1994), *Civil Rights: Leading Cases* (Little, Brown, 1980), and *Shade of Brown: New Perspectives on School Desegregation* (Teachers College Press, 1980). Bell has developed his views in greater detail in *Silent Covenants:* Brown v. Board *and the Quest for Racial Justice* (Oxford University Press, 2004).

A. WADE BOYKIN

A. Wade Boykin is an expert in the field of psychology and codirector of the Center for Research on the Education of Students Placed at Risk (CRESPAR) at Howard University, a U.S. Department of Education–funded national research and development center jointly operating from Howard University and Johns Hopkins University. CRESPAR's mission is to formulate, implement, research, evaluate, and disseminate comprehensive school reform initiatives according to a "talent development" model of schooling. Professor Boykin and his colleagues received one of the largest grants ever for research on urban and minority education continuing since 1994. A graduate of Hampton University, he has taught psychology at Cornell University and was a fellow at the Center for Advanced Study in the Behavioral Sciences, Palo Alto, California, and a Spencer Fellow of the National Academy of Education. Professor Boykin has served as a professor and director of the psychology graduate program at Howard.

An accomplished writer, Professor Boykin was the coeditor of *Research Directions of Black Psychologists* (Russell Sage Foundation, 1979), is coauthor of the forthcoming *The Psychology of African Americans Experiences: An Integrity-Based Perspective,* and is coeditor of the forthcoming *Promoting High Achievement among All Children: Evidence-Based Programs, Practices and Procedures.*

KAHLIL GIBRAN CHISM

 Kahlil Gibran Chism received his B.A. in history, and his M.Ed. in secondary education and social studies, both from the University of Virginia at Charlottesville. He has taught American studies, U.S. history, world history, U.S. government, English, writing, and Spanish, all at the secondary level. As a graduate student at the University of Virginia, he taught introductions to classroom computer technology at the Curry School of Education.

Although he is certified and licensed as a classroom teacher, Mr. Chism currently serves as an education specialist in the Department of Museum Programs, National Archives and Records Administration, Washington, D.C. He assists in presenting a program of workshops, presentations, seminars, and nationwide videoconferences to a wide range of school and family audiences. Many of his workshops focus on the effective use and critical analysis of primary source materials. Mr. Chism researches, compiles, and drafts educational materials and authentic assessment activities for upper elementary through secondary school classrooms, using National Archives records. He has written "Teaching with Documents" articles for *Social Education,* the journal for the National Council of Social Studies, *Cobblestone,* a history publication for ten- to fourteen-year-olds, and various research articles and lessons for publication within the Digital Classroom section of the National Archives Web site.

Mr. Chism also has served as a research assistant and seminars facilitator for the Thomas Jefferson Foundation, the owners and operators of Monticello, the home of Thomas Jefferson. While at Monticello, Mr. Chism facilitated professional development seminars for high school history teachers, prepared special focus tours for K–12, university-level, and special-interest groups, and helped analyze and reinterpret the employee training manual and policies for all historical interpreters.

Mr. Chism is most proud of his work as a board member of the Community Teachers Institute, a not-for-profit organization that encourages, supports, and creates partnerships among higher education institutions, public school districts, and community organizations, to improve the effectiveness of public education by increasing the numbers of high-caliber, culturally-connected teachers in K–12 classrooms.

ISHMAIL CONWAY

Ishmail Conway, a third-generation educator, received his B.A. from Hampton Institute, his M.A. from the New School for Social Research, and his Ph.D. from the University of Virginia. He is currently an assistant professor in the Curry School of Education and a lecturer in the Drama Department. He has served in a variety of professional roles at Virginia Union University, Virginia Commonwealth University, and at Cornell. In 1993 the Association of College Unions-International selected Dr. Conway as the Multicultural Educator of the Year.

Dr. Conway has been a visiting lecturer at the Université De Cheikh Anta Diop (formerly the University of Dakar), Dakar, Senegal; high schools and training centers in Gambia and Senegal; Aquinas College; University of Arizona; Jackson State University; Howard University; Hampton University; University of Kansas; University of North Carolina, Wilmington and Charlotte; North Carolina A&T State University; North Carolina State University; College of William and Mary; Old Dominion University; James Madison University; Longwood College; Colonial Williamsburg Foundation; New York City Economic Development Council's "Open Doors Project" in New York City high schools; the National Alliance of Business Youth Motivation Task Force; and Virginia Commission for the Arts. "Dr. C," as he's known by students, is a popular choice on university campuses and conferences as a motivational speaker. He also has worked and consulted for several *Fortune* 500 corporations.

As a youth he performed with Duke Ellington's orchestra and appeared in several operas. Conway has performed in films for the

Colonial Williamsburg and Valley Forge Foundations and PBS, and is known for his directing work in theaters across Virginia and beyond.

"Central Virginia Dreamkeepers: Narratives of African American Teachers Who Taught before, during, and after the *Brown v. Topeka Board of Education* Decision" was his doctoral dissertation.

MARY HATWOOD FUTRELL

Mary Hatwood Futrell is an internationally known educator with a long list of credentials. Edward Boyer, former president of the Carnegie Foundation for the Advancement of Teaching, said that "the nation is deeply in debt to [her] for the clarity of her voice and for her commitment to both equity and excellence for our children."

Dr. Futrell is the former president of the National Education Association and former president of the World Confederation of Organizations of the Teaching Profession.

Currently she is dean of the Graduate School of Education and Human Development at her alma mater, George Washington University. Dr. Futrell has penned scores of journal articles and coauthored *Cannon's Concise Guide to Rules of Order* (Author's Choice Press, 2001).

CHERYL BROWN HENDERSON

Cheryl Brown Henderson is one of the three daughters of the late Reverend Oliver L. Brown, who, in the fall of 1951 along with twelve other families, led by attorneys for the NAACP, filed suit against the local Board of Education on behalf of their children. The case made its way all the way to the U.S. Supreme Court and on May 17, 1954, became known as the landmark decision, *Brown v. The Board of Education of Topeka, Kansas.* This case was named for Oliver Brown, i.e., *Oliver L. Brown et. al. vs. The Board of Education of Topeka.* Brown died in 1961 before knowing the impact this case would have on the country.

Cheryl is currently serving as president and CEO of the Brown Foundation for Educational Equity, Excellence, and Research. She is owner of Brown & Brown Associates, an educational consulting firm. She has extensive background in education, business, and civic leadership, having served on and chaired various local, state, and national boards. In addition, she has nearly two decades of experience in political advocacy, public policy implementation, and federal legislative development. She is also an associate with the Westerly Group, a public advocacy firm in Washington, D.C.

Cheryl's education includes a bachelor's degree in elementary education and mathematics from Baker University, Baldwin City, Kansas, a master's degree in guidance and counseling from Emporia State University, Emporia, Kansas, and an honorary doctorate of humane letters from Washburn University. She is the recipient of various awards and recognition for work in education and community service; presentations at numerous conferences and conventions; and for her work with Congress and the National Park Service to preserve sites associated with the landmark U.S. Supreme Court ruling of 1954.

In 1988 she founded the Brown Foundation. Since its establishment, this organization has provided scholarships to forty minority students; presented awards to local, state and national leaders; and sponsored programs on diversity and educational issues for some four thousand people. In 1990, under her leadership, the foundation successfully worked with the U.S. Congress to establish the Brown v. Board of Education National Park in Topeka, scheduled to open in late 2003. In 2001, also under her leadership, the foundation successfully worked with the U.S. Congress to establish the Brown v. Board of Education fiftieth Anniversary Presidential Commission, which will serve to provide a federal presence in the 2004 anniversary of the *Brown* decision.

On January 17, 1994, May 19, 1995, and May 2003 she was one of a group of individuals invited to a reception at the White House in honor of Dr. King and the Children of Civil Rights Movement, the 75th Anniversary, U.S. Department of Labor, Women's Bureau, and 49th Anniversary of *Brown v. Board of Education,* respectively.

Named in 1991 one of the one hundred most influential people in Topeka, Ms. Brown Henderson became in 1996 the first African American woman from Kansas to run for the U.S. House of Representatives. She has published numerous articles and is an active lecturer on the state of education in the United States post-*Brown.*

EVELYN HU-DEHART

Head of the Center for the Study of Race and Ethnicity at Brown University, Evelyn Hu-DeHart has reexamined the cultural dynamics of Asian Americans within the United States. The former professor and chair of Ethnic Studies and former director of the Center for Studies of Ethnicity and Race in America at the University of Colorado at Boulder, she has written several articles on the positioning of Asian Americans as the "model minority" and how that perception affects race relations among Asians, blacks, and whites.

Considered "one of the pillars of the ethnic studies movement in the U.S.," Ms. Hu-DeHart is author of the following books: *Across the Pacific: Asian Americans and Globalization (Asian American History and Culture)* (Temple University Press, 2000), *Yaqui Resistance and Survival: The Struggle for Land and Autonomy 1821–1910* (University of Wisconsin Press, 1984), and *Missionaries, Miners, and Indians* (University of Arizona Press, 1981).

James M. Jones

James M. Jones is professor of psychology at the University of Delaware and director of the Minority Fellowship Program at the American Psychological Association. Dr. Jones earned a B.A. from Oberlin College (1963); an M.A. from Temple University (1967); and his Ph.D. in social psychology from Yale University (1970). He was on the faculty of the Social Relations Department at Harvard University (1970–1976), during which time the first edition of his *Prejudice and Racism* (1972) was published, and he spent a year in Trinidad and Tobago on a Guggenheim Fellowship studying calypso humor. This work led to the development of the TRIOS model of the psychology of African American culture. McGraw-Hill published a second edition of *Prejudice and Racism* in 1997. Dr. Jones is currently working on a book on the cultural psychology of African Americans for Westview Press. Dr. Jones is a social psychologist, and serves on several editorial boards, including the *International Journal of Intercultural Relations* and the *Journal of Black Psychology,* and is past president of the Society of Experimental Social Psychology. He was awarded the 1999 Lifetime Achievement Award of the Society for the Psychological Study of Ethnic Minority Issues (Division 45) of the American Psychological Association, and the 2001 Kurt Lewin Award by the Society for the Psychological Study of Social Issues (Division 9).

Charles J. Ogletree Jr.

Prominent legal theorist and Harvard Law School professor Charles J. Ogletree Jr., recipient of honorary degrees from Amherst College and North Carolina Central, Wilberforce, and Miami Universities, among other universities, has been described as someone who "has never forgotten his roots" by Donald A. Thigpen, president of the Washington Bar Association. Ogletree first received national attention for his representation of Professor Anita Hill during the confirmation hearings for Justice Clarence Thomas.

Dr. Ogletree has received national attention for spearheading the lawsuit against the U.S. government and specific American corporations that benefited from free labor, for reparations owed to descendants of enslaved Africans. Dr. Ogletree coauthored *Beyond the Rodney King Story: An Investigation of Police Conduct in Minority Communities* (Northeastern University Press, 1995), and is the author of a critique of *Brown v. Board of Education* on its fiftieth anniversary, *All Deliberate Speed* (W. W. Norton, 2004).

GARY ORFIELD

As codirector of the Civil Rights Project at Harvard University, Gary Orfield has dedicated his time and career to obtaining equality within America's public school systems. He served on the research staff of the Brookings Institute in Washington and served as a scholar in residence at the U.S. Commission on Civil Rights. His work was cited in the 2003 Supreme Court decision on upholding affirmative action.

A court-appointed expert in school desegregation cases, Dr. Orfield is currently professor of education and social policy at Harvard Graduate School of Education.

Dr. Orfield has written several books on civil rights in schools and colleges, including *Dismantling Desegregation: The Quiet Reversal of Brown v. Board of Education* (New Press, 1997), *Raising Standards or Raising Barriers?: Inequality and High Stakes Testing in Public Education* (Century Foundation Press, 2001), *The Closing Door: Conservative Policy and Black Opportunity* (University of Chicago Press, 1993), and *Diversity Challenged* (Harvard Education Press, 2002).

MARCO PORTALES

Marco Portales is a professor of English at Texas A&M University. Since arriving in College Station in 1991, following faculty appointments at the University of Houston, Clear Lake (1979–1991) and the University of California, Berkeley (1974–1979), he has taught graduate and under-graduate courses in American ethnic literature and in the life and literature of the Southwest.

Professor Portales received his B.A. in English from the University of Texas at Austin in 1970 and his Ph.D. in English, with a specialization in American literature, in 1974 from the State University of New York, Buffalo.

At Texas A&M he has served as English undergraduate director (1992–1993), as acting director of the Race and Ethnic Studies Institute (RESI) (1993–1994), and as executive assistant to the president (1996–1997). Between 1986 and 1988 he served as dean of Arts and Sciences at Texas Southmost College in Brownsville. In that position he helped launch the first successful $3 million endowment drive for the college, in 1987.

Professor Portales was elected president of the international Society for the Study of the Multi-Ethnic Literature of the United States (MELUS) (1992–1994), having previously served as secretary, program chair, and reader for *MELUS,* the organization's journal, currently published at the University of Connecticut, Storrs.

Aside from publishing seventeen refereed articles and twenty-one other articles, Professor Portales published a book, *Youth and Age in American Literature* (Peter Lang, 1989). In 2000 Temple University Press published his *Crowding Out Latinos: Mexican Americans in the Public Consciousness,* an interdisciplinary study that discusses the impact of education, the media, Chicano literature, given today's demographic changes concerning U.S. Latinos and American society.

With his wife, Rita, Portales has a 272-page book manuscript

"Quality Education for Latinos: Print and Oral Skills for ALL Students, K–College" under contract with the University of Texas Press. Separately he has prepared forty-four essays for a book, *Latino Sun, Rising: Our Spanish-Speaking U.S. World,* that will be published in 2004 by the Texas A&M University Press.

THEODORE M. SHAW

Theodore M. Shaw is the president and director-counsel of the NAACP Legal Defense and Educational Fund, Inc. (LDF), and has directed LDF's education docket and litigated school desegregation, capital punishment, and other civil rights cases at the trial and appellate levels, as well as in the U.S. Supreme Court. Mr. Shaw was lead counsel, representing African American and Latino student-intervenors in the University of Michigan undergraduate school affirmative action case, in which the Supreme Court ruled in 2003 in favor of the compelling state interest of diversity.

Formerly a trial attorney in the civil rights division of the United States Department of Justice, Mr. Shaw litigated school desegregation and housing discrimination cases, and was awarded a special commendation for outstanding service. He established a western regional office of LDF in Los Angeles, where he also litigated housing discrimination and voting rights cases.

Mr. Shaw has served on the law school faculties at the University of Michigan, Columbia University, Temple University, and CUNY.

He has testified before Congress and before state legislatures, been a frequent guest on television and radio programs, and published numerous newspaper, magazine, and law review articles. As a participant of the Affirmative Action Affinity Group with the International Human Rights Group, he has fostered public support and offered litigation strategies for equality in Brazil, Uruguay, South Africa, Switzerland, Hungary, Bulgaria, and Chile.

TAVIS SMILEY

Some would say that an exclusive interview with the president of the United States during one of the most controversial scandals to ever hit the White House is the interview of a lifetime. Others would say interviewing Fidel Castro in the wake of unprecedented U.S. sanctions relief or the conversation with Pope John Paul II was the most significant.

Host of *The Tavis Smiley Show from NPR,* Smiley is the first African American to host his own signature talk show in the history of National Public Radio. For the ABC Radio Network, Smiley hosts *The Smiley Report,* heard daily on urban contemporary radio stations across the United States, and appears twice weekly on the *Tom Joyner Morning Show.* In addition, Mr. Smiley has his own imprint (Smiley Books) with Hay House to create a series of products including empowerment cards, audiocassettes, mini-books, and success seminars. Smiley was previously the host of the award-winning *BET TONIGHT with Tavis Smiley.*

Mr. Smiley has authored six books. His most recent, *Keeping the Faith: Stories of Love, Courage, Healing and Hope from Black America,* is an inspiring collection of personal narratives about love, loss, and faith by African Americans from all walks of life.

Mr. Smiley is founder of the Tavis Smiley Foundation, a nonprofit organization, whose mission is to encourage, empower, and enlighten black youth. Youth to Leaders (Y2L), the cornerstone program of the foundation, is an annual series of one-day leadership-building conferences that take place in cities across the United States. *Tavis Smiley Presents,* a subsidiary of The Smiley Group, Inc., was created to bring ideas and people together through symposiums, seminars, forums, and town hall meetings.

A graduate of Indiana University, Mr. Smiley was previously a top aide to former Los Angeles mayor Tom Bradley, and has since provided analysis on everything from C-SPAN to PBS, and the *Today* show to *World News Tonight with Peter Jennings.* Mr. Smiley's advocacy work has been profiled on *60 Minutes.*

One of ten children, Mr. Smiley is single and lives Los Angeles. In his spare time, Mr. Smiley enjoys a good game of Scrabble with friends.

JUAN WILLIAMS

 Juan Williams has been national correspondent, editorial writer, and political columnist for the past twenty-three years for the *Washington Post.* Currently the senior correspondent for National Public Radio News, Mr. Williams is the author of the best-selling book (which accompanied the PBS television documentary series of the same title) *Eyes on the Prize: America's Civil Rights Years, 1954–1965* (Penguin USA, 1988), which won him critical acclaim and an Emmy award. He also penned a biography, *Thurgood Marshall: American Revolutionary* (Times Books, 2000). David K. Shipler of the *New York Times Book Review* described Mr. Williams's biography as "a strong piece of journalism crammed with fascinating detail, done in an unassuming style driven by the factual narrative."

Mr. Williams's new work, *This Far by Faith: Stories from the African-American Religious Experience* (William Morrow, 2003), chronicles the deep connection black Americans have with Christianity and the church.

RICHARD L. WRIGHT

 Richard L. Wright, professor of linguistics in the School of Communications and chairman of the Faculty Senate at Howard University, is a native of Washington, D.C. Educated in the district's public schools, he subsequently attended Howard University, from which he graduated in 1964, having participated actively as a student in the civil rights struggles being coordinated from this campus. He received a Fulbright grant to study in Guatemala for the 1964–1965 academic year, following which he completed his master's and Ph.D. degrees in linguistics at the University of Texas in Austin in 1971 and 1976, respectively. His primary areas of research and publication are in the field of sociolinguistics, specifically in early language learning, social and psychological factors in language development and language use, assessing language ability across grades, sociocultural dynamics in language use, African American language dynamics, and effective literacy.

INDEX